Project management: getting it right

Arnold P Reid

CRC Press
Boca Raton Boston New York Washington, DC

WOODHEAD PUBLISHING LIMITED

Cambridge England

Published by Woodhead Publishing Limited, Abington Hall, Abington, Cambridge
CB1 6AH, England

Published in North and South America by CRC Press LLC, 2000 Corporate Blvd, NW
Boca Raton FL 33431, USA

First published 1999, Woodhead Publishing Ltd

British Library Cataloguing in Publication Data
A catalogue record for this book is available from the British Library.

Library of Congress Cataloging in Publication Data
A catalog record for this book is available from the Library of Congress.

Woodhead Publishing ISBN 1 85573 420 6
CRC Press ISBN 0-8493-0645-0
CRC Press order number: WP0645

Cover design by The ColourStudio
Typeset by Best-set Typesetter Ltd, Hong Kong
Printed by TJ International, Cornwall, England

To my wife, Gavina

Contents

Preface

For over 20 years, I have been involved in Planning and Cost Control, from engineer to Corporate Planning Manager, working with and for a number of major companies. I mention this fact not as an authority for the book, but simply to say that in that time, I have seen and tried most of what were then, and to some extent still are, new ideas and methods.

Many of those successful ideas led to the development of techniques that are taken for granted today. On the other hand, there were a number of ideas and techniques which failed – they appeared to be good, were well presented, discussed in some detail, and looked logical and feasible at the time but, in practice, they were to prove unworkable for many reasons. I am not blameless in this respect because some of those ideas were my own!

A few of the mistakes made related to the technical aspects of the work, which were and still are, to a great extent, a mechanical process. Most mistakes related to the way the work was managed, and were probably caused by lack of experience and the fact that we were too lenient on the demands we made on other companies. We may be excused for this to a certain extent as we were attempting to develop new, or at least better, planning and cost techniques, techniques which would cope with highly technical and complex projects, with costs in the hundreds of millions.

The tools at our disposal were less sophisticated then – computers which are now the mainstay of the industry, were relatively new to the profession, and the supporting software was very limited in its application and not very user-friendly. As for works of technical reference, they consisted of a number of books on networking techniques but none on how to manage the planning and cost control aspects of a multimillion dollar offshore or onshore project.

Even today, there is still a limited number of books which can be referenced on the subject and fewer still which deal with the practical application of planning and cost control management techniques. This new book will, I hope, rectify that to some extent and become a useful reference for managers and young engineers alike by helping the reader with the day-today management and practical application of planning and cost engineering and their interrelationships with other key disciplines.

I would like to thank Roland Cantu for reviewing the book and Craig Gilbert and David Blaney for encouraging me to write it.

Introduction

The techniques which are described in the book are those in use on many major projects today. Like most techniques they will have variations and modifications to suit the particular project and management style. Some of the techniques described with regards to the software integration are only now being used on such projects as the USA space station. Others mentioned in the book may be regarded as common and standard planning and cost techniques.

One of my problems in writing this book was on how best to present the information. To use a standard book format, if there is such a thing, would possibly make the book too long and laborious to read. After giving the problem some thought, I opted for a semi-procedural approach, minimum words, maximum information. Most managers are familiar with this technique and it will give to those not familiar with procedure development a practical example of presentation and content.

Industrial management in general has realised for many years that good forward planning, budget control and performance measurement are essential elements in maintaining the viability of any project. Only by exercising that control can they hope to attain the project efficiency which is fundamental in maintaining profitability and the meeting of contract schedule targets.

When we look at the control disciplines more closely, to understand what is required in order to achieve the project goals, there are three key elements which are essential to success.

The quality of the people who are involved	• Good people
Knowing exactly what has to be done	• Defined scope
Guidance as to how the work has to be done	• Procedures

Who does it, what has to be done and how is it to be done?

There are also the 'when' and 'where' issues. It is the function of schedule to establish the 'when'. The 'where' of course is dictated by the project location and the contract awards.

The importance of people

I mentioned good people. They are our most precious resource as they are a prerequisite for any task or function to be effective. All the company procedures, technical aids, computers and so on are only so much inert material without the right people to use and operate them.

It is therefore the manager's first task to pull together the core personnel of a suitable project team. This function requires the selection of the right people for the job: people with the skills and experience and more importantly, the dedication necessary for the anticipated tasks ahead. It is never an easy task to make the selection with any degree of confidence unless those doing the selection have a detailed knowledge of the work to be undertaken. Only in this way can a proper suitability assessment be made of any individual. This is only common sense but unfortunately common sense is not all that common and therefore it does not always happen.

Someone may have the technical experience required for the post but have flaws in their personality which make them unsuitable or vice versa. It is for this reason that, when hiring new staff particularly for a technical post, major companies usually insist on having at least two interviews, the technical interview to assess the candidate's skills and abilities and the personnel interview to assess the domestic and psychological elements. Of course, it is always possible to put a square peg in a round hole, if the square peg is small enough and has the ability to expand to fill the new shape tightly. This is often done when we give someone a new opportunity.

What has to be done?

The quality of the planning and cost estimates which we are able to produce depends largely on the information available; not only the volume of information but also the clarity of the instruction on management policies with regard to procedures and interdepartmental communication. It is important that management ensures that communication channels remain open between departments and functions so that the maximum information is available on which to base the plan and cost estimate, and to update them when it becomes necessary.

The company yardstick

The company and all departments and functions within the company will be judged to a large extent on how well they perform against the schedule and budget as these provide a yardstick for company performance measurement. It is therefore unwise to restrict access to information or prevent the full co-operation of any department in the planning and cost operation.

It is incumbent on the planning and cost engineer to make the best use of these channels, to solicit information and reach agreement on the logic and activity elements within the plan.

How is it to be done?

The guidelines come in the form of procedures, and the first question to ask is why should we have them. The answer is simple. The object of a procedure is to ensure that, through approved working routines and standardisation of approach, staff can integrate their work with other sections of planning or cost engineering whether in-house or external. Planning procedures, for example, **when observed** allow compatibility of output and aggregation of sub-networks, resources etc. resulting in an overall increase in efficiency. Where there are new members of staff or juniors under training, procedures not only educate but assist in preventing costly mistakes. The value of good **practical** procedures cannot be overestimated.

Good procedures should be designed to allow a degree of flexibility but still retain all the management control instructions. No two projects are exactly alike and therefore flexibility allows adaptation to meet the specific needs of a particular project. Flexibility also makes the procedures more acceptable to the staff who must work to them and this enhances the degree of conformity. It is essential that the fundamental management elements within any procedure are maintained. To ensure maximum conformity the company must be prepared to conduct an audit and examine any new project procedure for variances. This establishes the effect of any variance which could impact on the company or project in a negative way. Should this occur, steps would naturally need to be taken to rectify the matter.

The diversity of today's management structures and the complexity of today's major projects have created the need for control procedures to be written. There is a need not only to let company employees know how to perform their work but also to let potential clients or contractors know how the work is to be performed. When it becomes necessary to prepare a procedure there are two goals to aim for:

- To create a standard to work to that everyone understands.
- To develop a method of accomplishing a task that is documented in past project history, and in this way, avoid repetitive mistakes.

In the beginning

Before moving further there is a need to put things in order to give a better perspective of the various elements and functions we will be dealing with throughout the book. To do this effectively we need to take into consideration the development of a project from concept to conclusion. What will be needed at each stage of project life and how will it impact on that particular phase? In this way we should be able to evaluate the validity of our decisions and the reason for taking specific actions.

How often do we wonder why a particular decision is made, when we can see no rhyme or reason for it? Later, when more information becomes available we see the justification for the decision when we are able to view the 'big picture'. What follows will, I hope, give you the tools you need to see not only the big picture but to see it on an all-round screen!

1
Project need

1.1 Project need

All projects exist because of a need – the need to expand, take advantage
of a commercial situation, improve the environment or whatever. What they
all have in common is another type of *need* and that is the need to complete the project as efficiently as possible. Efficiency in this respect focuses
on the efficient use of time and resources both physical and monetary.

Once the idea of a venture exists so also does the embryo of the project.
When enough people with the ability to allocate funds are interested, the
next step is to investigate the prospect more fully.

We first become aware of the seriousness of the intention when the bones
of the idea arrive on our desk. This is normally accompanied by the instruction to put together a number of options/scenarios complete with programme and cost analysis. If a company is about to invest large sums of
money, they want the best option for success in terms of the facility and
risk. Under normal circumstances there will be three main stages of selection and approval before the actual project is approved.

Conceptual study

The conceptual study will look at the various possibilities and solutions that
may be applied to the prospect, and also the general viability. The analysis
at this stage will be very broad brush, allowing comparisons of the various
concepts. This would be accompanied by a brief scenario prepared by the
design, construction and engineering departments to highlight the various
pros and cons as they see them. Assuming that the project is viable, one or
possibly two of the conceptual proposals will warrant a feasibility study
being conducted.

Feasibility study

The feasibility study will look in much more detail at the proposal selected,
improving on the plan, cost, engineering, procurement, etc, to see if it is

achievable. The project would be promoted to the development stage if a feasibility study proved its practicality, established that the associated risks were within acceptable limits and assumed that the monetary investment could be found. In time, after a bit of double checking, hybridising of ideas and commercial evaluation, one option, if it was found to be viable, would get the amber light and move on to a more detailed development phase. I say amber light simply because until a development has full partner approval, it cannot get the green light.

Development/project stage

The development or project stage would advance the feasibility study from an 'idea' on paper through to a three-dimensional working entity. Before the development/project stage can be reached, a number of analysis phases need to be conducted. The analysis is seldom, if ever, a one department function, it requires the co-operation of all departments, each with their own specialised knowledge and input to the various options.

To perform these tasks and to piece together viable concepts requires the use of historical data stored from previous projects. The more abundant the historical data, the more accurate will be the conceptual estimates. The need for gathering and collating historical data cannot be stressed too strongly. A thousand pounds spent on gathering data can, and has in many cases, saved millions. Lack of this type of data has resulted too often in losses of the same magnitude. **In simple terms poor data, poor estimate, poor chance of success.**

Before arriving at a decision as to which prospect or prospects should be taken further, the risks involved have to be further evaluated. There is also a need to make the right decision based on the facts and probabilities presented. Fortunately, one or two tried and tested techniques can be used to assist us in our endeavours – decision trees and risk analysis.

1.2   Decision trees

In business there are always decisions to be made, some of them simple and others complicated. The simple ones seldom present a problem but the complicated variety where there are risks, various options, and numerous end results, can and do present a major problem. In these cases, any aid which will facilitate the right decision is something we should get to know about.

What then is a decision tree? It is simply an analytical tool which requires a diagram to be drawn showing the sequential decision choices, see Fig. 1.1.

A decision tree is normally drawn from left to right, with angles and line lengths inserted as the 'drawer' dictates. What is important is that the node

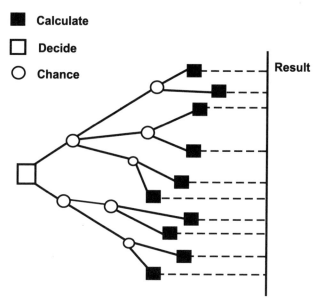

1.1   Decision tree.

points are defined according to their type. The symbols used to denote type are again arbitrary.

There are normally three basic types of node. First the **decision node** where a decision needs to be made on which route to follow. Next the **chance node**, where there is more than one outcome probability. Where possible, these would not only state the probability of success but also the financial implications, i.e.: success 40% (0.4) + £50000, break-even 30% (0.3) £0, failure 30% (0.3) – £60000. The third node is the **point of calculation**. From this node the result of the decisions made to this point can be calculated. This is important when the tree is extensive.

The end result for each path chosen can be calculated and presented in a results column. What emerges with this sort of analysis is that taking the positive path on all occasions does not always give the best overall result. As in life, losing a little at some point may gain a lot in the end. In other words, a high risk hurdle, once overcome, can put you on a much better path.

In practice, the decision tree can be an ideal tool used in the context of a decision-making meeting. Not only do you get a maximum input to the analysis, which improves the quality of the result, but agreement with the end result is more widespread.

The benefits of this type of analysis are fairly straightforward. The discipline of conducting the analysis forces us to look more closely at the factors involved. The risks involved can be more clearly assessed with regard to the probability and financial outcome. Higher quality decision-making, based on a logical system of assessment, is the end result.

1.3   Cost aversion

This is a subject we all know about but which is seldom if ever mentioned in business other than in an offhand way. For example, you are asked to put a pound in a kitty for a bet on a horse, and you are aware that the odds are 50 to 1. This is not a problem to the average person; you may lose a pound, but if the horse wins, you win £50. If, on the other hand, you were asked to put £100 on a horse, you would think a lot more about it, and you would be looking for safer odds.

Again, if you were asked to put on a bet of £20000 which would mean a second mortgage on your house, you would want some very strong guarantees of its success, that is, if you had the courage to put on the bet in the first place. If, on the other hand, you were a multi-millionaire, you might feel no differently from the person placing the original one pound bet.

In simple terms, we only have an aversion to spending money if it is likely to impact adversely on our funds, now or in the future, and if there is a risk involved, we want to be sure that it is worth taking for the financial gain. The risk one person takes may vary from another depending on what he or she can afford to lose.

In business the same basic rules apply. You may have a sound prospect with what you consider a limited risk and a good return for the capital investment, but have difficulty in finding investors/partners. Assuming that the prospect is sound, the reason for lack of investment may simply be cost aversion.

You may think that large corporations have adequate funds for almost anything but this is just not so. Large corporations have their own projects to fund and therefore any remaining capital requires to be invested judiciously.

It would be nice to be able to quantify accurately in some way what may be termed **the preference to place funds** and no doubt some mathematician somewhere will define it. There are a few theories in existence but, in the author's experience, it is more likely to be based on emotional factors than on logical ones.

Figure 1.2 simply states that as the risk increases the less one is prepared to invest. Figure 1.3 simply states that the more money we have the less value it has (utility value). As to the curve and the axis values they would only be good for one individual/company and at one time if they could be relied upon. Too many other factors would have to be considered, i.e. the

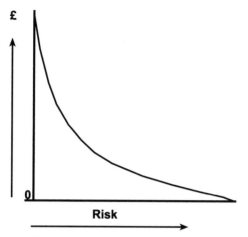

1.2   Risk aversion.

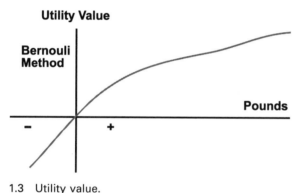

1.3   Utility value.

state of the market, recent investments along the same lines, other commitments and so on. We could probably say that a low investment with low risk and high profitability has a 90% chance of attracting a project investor. A high-investment, high-risk, low-profit project has a 1% or less chance of finding an investor.

1.4   Risk analysis

We have mentioned risk on several occasions so far. My pocket dictionary defines risk as 'the chance of possible harm' and chance may be defined as 'probability'. With any endeavour, there are a number of possible outcomes and as an investor we would want to know the probability of achieving a successful outcome before committing funds. Today no major, or for that matter minor project, would be entered into unless a probability analysis was conducted to establish the risk element involved.

Probability as such falls into two categories: subjective and objective. Subjective probability is when facts are few and guesswork and opinion are at their highest. Needless to say, the risk of failure is also at its highest. Objective probability is when there is empirical experience to draw on or when a discrete set of outcomes is likely. In this case, the risk element is reduced commensurate with the facts available.

Probability theory looks at the various events and the possible outcomes and, after numerous iterations, attempts to predict the frequency of any or all the outcomes. The technique is not infallible but it does allow us to estimate the odds of success within acceptable limits.

Today, with the software programs available we do not have to remember such techniques as chi-squared, null hypothesis, Poisson or binomial distribution relationships, and Monte Carlo can remain just another gambling town. The computer will deal with various methods and do the calculations more accurately and more quickly. As to conducting hundreds or thousands of iterations to obtain a reasonable confidence factor, there is just not the time available to do it manually; we again need to fall back on the computer to do the number crunching.

We do, however, need to have an understanding of frequency distribution and to be able to select a distribution which is representative of the anticipated outcome. We can look at a duration or a cost, for example, and from our historical data establish an average or mode. From this we can then make such statements as:

- We are unlikely to be more than 5% under that figure but we could go as much as 30% over.
- We consider it is possible with the state of the market to go 25% under that figure and no more than 10% over.
- Looking at the data, we could go 20% either way.

In these cases, we are using our experience and the data on hand to determine the shape of the distribution curve and to skew the curve according to our knowledge, see Fig. 1.4. Such a technique can prove highly successful, probably because it offers a good blend of theory and practice.

Two elements we need to consider in making our early judgements are performance and time which can impact on the probability of success.

In our initial evaluations, and before contracts are placed, all contractors are equal and therefore the probability results are similar in some ways to rolling dice to achieve a winning outcome. Once a contractor has been selected, their historical performance weights the dice according to that performance. A contractor with a good performance record would be similar to weighting the dice in favour of a winning result. The opposite would also

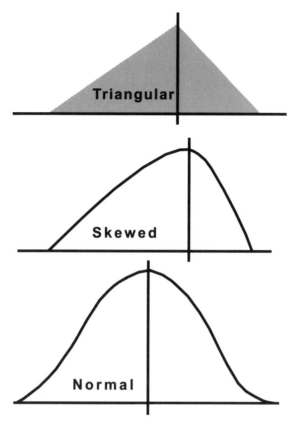

1.4   Distribution curves.

be true of a contractor with a lesser performance. The time span over which the analysis is taken also has a bearing on the outcome.

Let us look at two simple scenarios. Assume for a moment that you were to drive your car from your hotel to an office for a meeting which was only six minutes away. You pull out into the traffic and discover to your dismay there is an accident up ahead which is delaying the traffic. Your journey has taken nine minutes, you have a 50% overrun of time, and with the length of the journey, the legal speed restriction, etc, there was no way to make up the lost time. Fortunately, the three-minute delay made little or no impact on the meeting.

Now let us assume that you have a two-hour drive to the meeting with the same three-minute time loss. You would now have sufficient time remaining to cope with the delay and still arrive on time; also if you were late, the overrun is unlikely to be by 50%.

In practice, we find that the best results which reflect actual performance are obtained by considering a reasonable number of major elements covering the project scope, as opposed to a multitude of small components.

Computer software dealing with risk analysis normally works from a triangular distribution and with a set of data, as opposed to a data population. A population is defined as a large number of results/data from which the distribution curve is drawn. A set of data is a limited number of values which have been derived from a statistical population, i.e. minimum, maximum, most likely.

When dealing with a population, there are three terms that are used to describe the data within a population, median, mode and mean. It is worth reminding ourselves just what they represent, see Fig. 1.5.

- The mean is the sum of all the values divided by the number of values. This is termed the arithmetic mean or average; there are other means such as geometric, quadratic, etc., but unless stated, the mean is taken as the arithmetic mean.
- The median is the point in the centre of all values, there being an equal number of values greater and less than the median value.
- The modal or mode point is where the greatest number of one value occurs, i.e. the high point on the distribution curve.

While in no sense a treatise on probability, it is worth noting two rules in relation to probability that on occasions could impact on the analysis.

The **addition rule** states that the probability that one or another of two mutually exclusive events will occur is the sum of their separate possibilities – which must equal one. To make that statement a bit more easy to understand, a coin has a head and a tail (mutually exclusive – if you toss the coin you either get a head or a tail). Each time you toss the coin you have a 50/50 chance of a head or a tail. If you want a head and a tail you

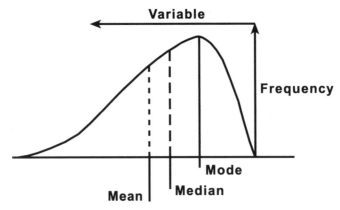

1.5   Distribution curve values.

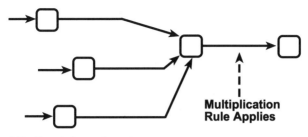

1.6 Event dependency.

do not have a 100% chance by tossing the coin twice. Because there are four possible solutions to two tosses of the coin, the likelihood of the combination that you would like to achieve therefore diminishes. Once you attach/add another desired outcome to a possibility, the addition reduces the possibility of success.

The **multiplication rule** applies where there are two or more events which have various outcomes. The events are in themselves independent but the results are dependent. An example of this would be the rolling of two dice and seeking an outcome of 7 (1 + 6 = 5.6%) (any combination = 16.7%).

The multiplication rule has a bearing on network activities where two or more activities require to be completed before another can start, see Fig. 1.6.

1.5   A question of truth

One area where real danger lies is in major first-time projects; they are notorious for having major overruns of both time and money. Two ventures which come quickly to mind are the Channel Tunnel and the first generation of offshore platforms. There are of course hundreds of major first-time projects in almost every country of the world which have suffered the same fate.

What did risk analysis tell us about these projects? Was risk not foreseen, or did somebody know and not speak out, for fear of losing investors? Were the projects so poorly managed that an overrun was inevitable? The truth is that **it was not apparent that they were grossly underestimated** simply because no true historical data existed on which to base the estimates. Hypothetical probability distributions 'just don't cut it', as they say in America.

The important point with major new ventures which are, to a large extent, charting new ground is to **be aware of the danger of major overruns and prepare for it**. A colleague of mine once said in his Southern accent, 'Why the hell with these new projects don't we let them crunch the numbers and when they've finished, we will just add 70%?' It was intended to be a frivolous remark but it carried a lot of truth, as history was to prove.

The earlier versions of North Sea offshore platforms had major budget and time problems but as construction performance history developed, the accuracy of planning and associated cost estimates steadily increased. Today, the offshore industry is regarded by many as having reached a state-of-the-art ability in both planning and estimating.

Getting it right depends more than anything else on using historical performance data. A few years back, I arrived at a company to take over the post of Corporate Planning Manager, and one of my first tasks was to look at a project which was having problems. The project was a semi-submersible drilling rig being built at a local shipyard. A visit to the yard, an examination of their recent performance, a few calculations done on the back of a business card (tonnes to erect divided by the average tonnes per month erected) and, true enough, the problem looked massive. My next action was to have the planning team look a bit more deeply at the problem, adding weather factors, running a probability analysis, interrogating the logic, etc, which indicated an 18-month overrun.

When I presented the results at the next management meeting, they were received with an air of incredulity, and my colleagues must have thought I was not putting enough water in my whisky! I must admit that I was wrong, since the project overran by 19 months!

No matter what the yard tried to do, they could not beat their history or overcome their PCC (performance control channel). It is a fact that once a construction yard is established and their performance over a period of time has been established, the yard can never better the production rate to any great extent. This may appear a harsh statement, though not intended to be, but it is a fact that has been proven over and over again. The reason for this is fairly simple. The yard's resources, if well managed, will be running at their best or near best performance. That performance may be improved here and there by increasing or improving the facilities but, when taken as a whole, the overall performance difference will be very small if it exists at all.

One of the main reasons for this is that a performance control channel (bottleneck to you and me!) exists, created when, somewhere along the line, components have to come together or be completed in a sequential order. In a fabrication yard this occurs during the erection/construction process. The component parts can be made all over the country but one day the final construction starts and the PCC is created. With an onshore process plant PCCs are created once you 'get out the ground', completing of the underground piping, cables, foundations and so on. The realisation of this fundamental truth will prevent the engineer or manager from becoming too optimistic when subjected to inspiring promises.

Assuming that the planning section has made a reasonable job preparing the logical assembly and that we allocated adequate resources, the production programme will be established and the rate of completion fixed within close limits. The sequencing of the work determines the work faces that can be worked on at one time; the workspace available and the techniques required limit the number of men and amount of equipment that may be used at the work face. The only other variable is time and it is normal to plan for one shift working on an onshore worksite and at least two-shift working offshore. In practice, by adding an additional shift, which often happens in times of trouble, the production advantage is normally very limited. This is due to the restrictions imposed by other functions, such as radiography, hydro-testing, acid cleaning and other similar support and QA/QC functions which have been scheduled to be carried out during the quieter period.

What we learn from all of this is to be realistic in our estimating, and to use established historical data. Estimates should not be changed because of performance improvements offered; one should wait until they are proven in fact. One should also be extra cautious with new products. Above all risk analysis should be carried out.

2
Feasibility study

2.1 Quantifying parameters

Once a concept looks as if it has the ability to meet the project criteria the next step is to see if it is really practical and that requires a more in-depth analysis. Within the feasibility study profile, many concepts will require to be firmed up and decisions made on major components and time parameters.

The task will be to look in some detail at the actual process that will be required, based on an estimate of the production levels anticipated. It is on these production levels that the whole project is based. In the case of an oil platform (see Fig. 2.1) the company will have spent a vast fortune on seismic surveys, test drilling and such like, to verify the size of the field, the reserves, and the quality and quantity of the reserve that can be removed. A process plant would have slightly different parameters – security of the process material and marketability of the end product. Only if these parameters, coupled with the available market and the anticipated market price at the planned production date, proved viable, would the project have been considered.

As quantifying parameters, the production rate quality and quantity will be fairly accurate. For the benefit of what follows, let us assume this is a gas platform and the production rate is around 400 to 500 thousand barrels (MBBL) per day of NGL.

The time and cost elements will be based on an estimate of the dry weight of each process module. The dry weight is the weight of pipes, vessels, etc, containing no fluids and the design will of course be based on the operating weight. To those not familiar with estimating major projects by weight this may appear rather a crude basis on which to estimate a multi-million pound/dollar project. In fact, it is very accurate due to the amount of historical data available, and the knowledge and experience of those undertaking the estimation. Knowledge and experience in this situation should

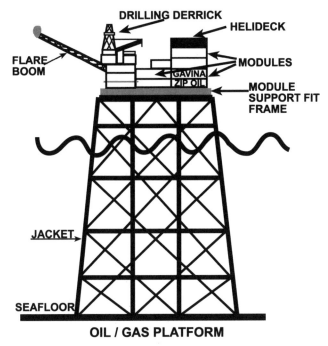

OIL / GAS PLATFORM

2.1   Platform components.

never be undervalued. Even with good data, no two projects are alike and there is a need for experienced integration of all the elements in order to visualise the coming together of all the component parts and the problems that may arise.

2.2   Component parts

At the feasibility stage we will still be in a 'best guess' situation although we will know the water depth, and to some extent will fix the steel jacket parameters coupled with the topside weight. To develop the early estimates reference would be made using estimating data graphs, as shown in Fig. 2.2 and 2.3. As for the topside, we will be able to estimate the weight of each major process but will not know exactly how many modules there will be, whether many small modules or a few very large modules containing a number of processes.

The bar chart in Fig. 2.4 shows a typical conceptual submission, of which there would be a number of different examples. For the purposes of the exercise, this concept will be the alternative selected.

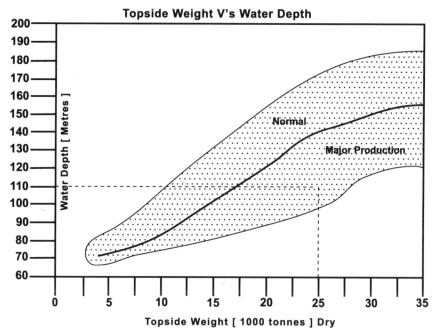

2.2   Topside estimating data graph.

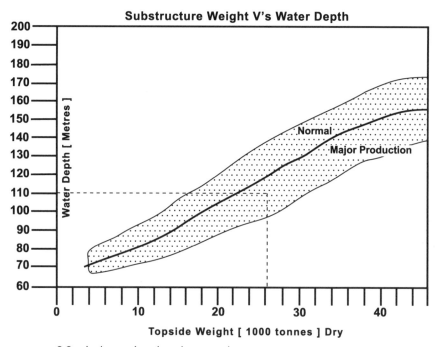

2.3   Jacket estimating data graph.

GAVINA FIELD			CONCEPTUAL STUDY				PROPOSAL 6 / 8
ACTIVITY	1994	1995	1996	1997	1998	1999	**Duration**
JACKET & PILES Design Procure Fabricate							14 24 28
TOPSIDE Design Procure Fabricate							24 32 29
INSTALLATION Jacket Topside							1 1
HOOK- UP & **COMM.**							14
Water Depth 100 Metres			Anticipated		Jacket and Piles 26,000 tonnes Topside 25,000 tonnes		

2.4   Bar chart.

Components conceptual estimate:

Module type	Module no.	Tonnes Approx. dry weight
Accommodation	01	2 500
Helideck	02	260
Drilling rig	03	1 240
Drilling facilities	04	3 800
Wellheads	05	1 800
Gas compression	06	3 000
Production/export	07	3 600
Utilities	08	1 200
Power generation	09	1 800
Communications and control	10	1 000
Integrated cellar deck	11	4 800
	Total	**25 000 tonnes**
Jacket structure	12	**26 000 tonnes**

What we now have is a breakdown of the major components as antici-pated from past experience, and dry weights derived from our historical data on similar projects. How close the breakdown of the components is to their actual weight will not become evident until the design work has been completed. Before that can happen, the project go-ahead will be given, and planning schedules and cost estimates will have been made on these weight estimates. Producing the weight estimates will be part engineering, part planning and part cost engineering.

Project management

In addition there will be the management breakdown to be added to the costs, again based mainly on historical data and a very few facts. The management costs would be based on a percentage of total structure costs and again at this stage the costs would be speculative.

2.3   Conceptual estimate, schedule and costs

The method used to estimate the final costs would be as shown on the cost-estimating flowsheet in Fig. 2.5.

The estimates made during the conceptual and feasibility phases in the case of (£/$) cost per tonne (CPT), man-hours per tonne (MPT) and tonnes per month (TPM) would be derived from a three-times estimate.

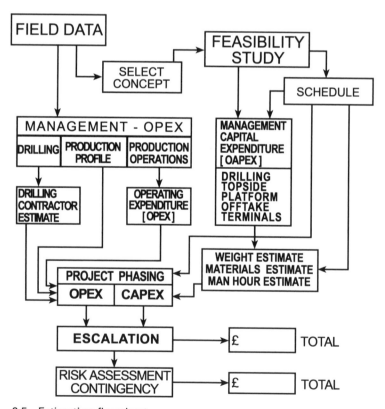

2.5   Estimating flowsheet.

Conceptual estimate

Man-hour estimate
Man-hour breakdown including directs and indirects excluding management, onshore construction

Module type	MPT	% TPM
Wellhead	155	13.8
Separation	164	6.3
Pipe line metering	150	5.3
Compression	155	6.0
Gas sales	150	4.8
Utilities	182	12.8
Power generation	153	3.4
Mud module	145	3.1
Central and work shops	184	4.6
Accommodation	174	10.5
Switch room	98	3.0
Cellar deck	256	6.2

Other topside component structures

Drilling substructure	80	1.8
Flare boom/tower	150	0.9
Helideck	136	0.9
Module support frame	144	14.6
External equipment	154	2.0
		100%

Overall weighted topside average = **157 MPT**

Overview rates conceptual estimating

Detail design	MPT	TPM
Jackets Concrete	1.5 to 2.1	NK (not known)
Steel – small (6 kt)	4.5 to 5.5	1000 to 1200
Steel – medium (15 kt)	4.2 to 5.2	1300 to 1450
Steel – large (20 kt plus)	4.0 to 5.0	1550 to 1860
Topside: on concrete jacket	60 to 70	
Not known		
on steel jacket	50 to 55 (Oil)	1000 to 1400
	45 to 50 (Gas)	

Construction	MPT	TPM
Jackets Steel – small	150	400 to 500
Steel – medium	150	700 to 800
Steel – large	150	850 to 1050
Topside on concrete	125	NK

on steel	50 to 170	105 (2000 t module)
		130 (3000 t module)
Accommodation modules	170 to 185	70
Total topside with multi-yard fabrication	820 to 900 TPM	
Offshore hook-up	42 to 48 (dry wt) 1600 to 1800	

Calculations

Topside   25 000 tonnes
  Design
  50 MPT = 1 250 000 man-hours
  Construct
  157 MPT = 3 925 000 man-hours
Jacket   26 000 tonnes
  Design
  5 MPT = 130 000 man-hours
  Construct
  150 MPT = 3 900 000 man-hours
  Topside hook-up 25 000 tonnes
  45 MPT = 1 125 000 man-hours
  Project management 51 000 tonnes
  60 MPT = 3 060 000 man-hours

Durations

Topside design 25 000 t at 1040 TPM = 24 months
  Procure at 780 TPM = 32 months
  Fabricate at 860 TPM = 29 months
Jacket design 26 000 t at 1860 TPM = 14 months
  Procure at 1080 TPM = 24 months
  Fabricate at 900 TPM = 29 months
Hook-up 25 000 t at 1780 TPM = 14 months

It should be realised that, for example, a hook-up contractor will only handle a small proportion of the physical weight, and that on every case, the TPM is a factor used to establish durations, man-hours, etc. At this stage of estimation, factors and durations would be rounded up or down.

A result of 31 months 2 weeks and 4 days or 2 400 121 man-hours is indicating an accuracy that just does not exist at this time, or for that matter at any time. To forecast any project to that degree does not need foresight, it needs some form of magic!

Cost estimate

(CPT – cost per ton)

Engineering/design topside 25 000 t
£900 CPT   = £22 500 000

Jacket 26000t
£200 CPT   = 5200000

Procurement/materials topside
£4500 CPT = £112500000

　　Jacket
£570 CPT   = 14820000

Construct　　Topside
£4200 CPT = £105000000

　　Jacket
£2000 CPT = 52000000

Install offshore 51000t
£1000 CPT = £51000000

Hook-up 25000t
£5500 CPT = £137500000

Total　　　 = £500520000

Project management 25%　　£125130000

Total = £625650000

This figure would form a base estimate exclusive of escalation and contingency as would all the other conceptual proposals. The factor for escalation and contingency would be the same for all and would be added as required to evaluate the overall project viability.

Total project breakdown	**Hist. %**	**Estimate %**
Project management	20	20.0
Engineering/design	5	4.5
Procurement/materials	20	20.35
Onshore construction	25	25.0
Offshore installation	8	8.15
Offshore construction	22	22.0
	100%	100%

What the conceptual figures indicate is that the breakdown is in the right 'ballpark' area. As for the estimated costs, they are again in keeping with the larger offshore platforms. Offshore platforms range from about £100 million for a smaller field to about £1 billion for the very large structures.

A point worth noting at this time with regard to the historical price is that, when preparing data for probabilistic analysis, the population costs must be escalated in line with today's costs. There is no point in mixing the cost of performing the work ten years ago, with samples from the same type of work today, and attempting to achieve an 'average'. You may think this is just common sense but, unfortunately, this is not always used, as has been proved on more than one occasion, and by people who you may think should have known better.

Process plants

In the case of process plants overall breakdowns can vary dramatically depending on the process and the location, therefore good 'like data' from projects of a similar size and type are necessary at this stage of development. A minimum type of breakdown would be as follows:

Overall cost percentage breakdown

Management	14.0%
Facilities	21.0%
Indirects	3.0%
Services	5.0%
Operating spares	0.75%
Others	0.51%
Equipment	26.9%
Civil	4.0%
Structural	2.0%
Electrical	4.0%
Piping	5.0%
Coatings	1.5%
Buildings	0.5%
	100%

Design and construction cost breakdown
Design

Civil	11.5%
Structural	5.0%
Mechanical	5.2%
Piping	33.0%
Electrical	8.6%
Instruments	18.5%
Process	8.6%
Telecom	0.6%
Vessels	0.9%
	100%

Construction

Mobilise and grade	3.8%
Structural steel foundations	4.7%

Equipment foundations	9.9%
Erect structural steel	7.9%
Erect equipment	14.7%
Underground piping	8.6%
Above-ground piping	12.4%
Mechanical tie-ins	3.8%
Underground conduit	4.4%
Above-ground conduit and cable	10.1%
Termination and testing	2.1%
Install instruments	8.8%
Terminate and test instruments	4.1%
Painting and insulation	2.5%
Commission/mechanical completion	2.2%
	100%

These breakdowns and later the sub-breakdowns of each element are the foundation stones of good cost and planning.

2.4   The strength of experience

It may appear to the reader that to prepare an estimate of this magnitude as simply as indicated even at the conceptual stage is just too easy. You might expect these estimates to be 200 pages long and full of all sorts of data, studies, etc. That in fact does not happen. Behind the simple rates used for calculation will be a large volume of data, in particular from engineering and procurement and based on the company's and other companies' experience. People taking the decisions will know just by looking at the results if they seem reasonable. The strength of their experience, for which there is no substitute, will enable them to identify any point which they feel does not look right. They will, of course, rightly demand and expect an explanation for these.

2.5   The feasibility expansion

The feasibility study will take the form of an expansion of all the elements within the conceptual study selected. The 'approval' of the concepts will allow all the company supporting departments to concentrate their efforts towards the possible new project, and much more relevant information on design, procurement and so on will become available to increase the accuracy of the study.

Jacket

As an example of this expansion we can look at the steel jacket and how it would be developed, see Fig. 2.6. At this point there would be no real hard

JACKET and MODULE SUPPORT FRAME

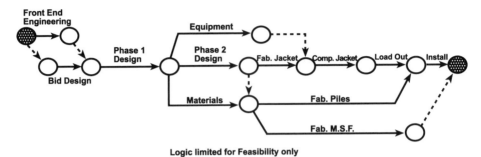

Logic limited for Feasibility only

2.6   Logic network arrows.

facts and therefore we need to rely on existing statistics to refine the estimate further.

Conceptual estimate 26 000 tonnes

This estimate would be further defined on a percentage basis as follows:

Bare jacket	55%	14 300 tonnes
Buoyancy tanks	12%	3 120
Cathodic protection	3%	780
Appurtenances	5%	1 300
Piles	25%	6 500
	Total	26 000 tonnes

Further examples of this sort of breakdown could be as follows:

Module support frame (cellar/integrated deck)

Conceptual estimate 4800 tonnes

MSF infill legs	14%	672 tonnes	(12–16%)
MSF section north	43%	2064	(40–45%)
MSF section south	43%	2064	(40–45%)
	Total	4800 tonnes	

Drilling facilities

Conceptual estimate 3800 tonnes

Skidding modules	14%	532	(10–18%)
Drilling modules	62%	2356	(60–65%)
Substructures	23%	874	(20–25%)
Annexe	1%	038	(0.5–1.5%)
	Total	3800 tonnes	

Wellheads

Conceptual estimate 1800 tonnes

Wellhead north	50%	900
Wellhead south	50%	900
	Total	1800 tonnes

In practice, the split would not be an exact 50% split; there would be a small variation of 3 to 5% of the total weight. At this time it is sufficient to indicate that the deck could be split roughly into two sections.

Gas compression

Conceptual estimate 3000 tonnes

Injection/compression two modules at 1500 tonnes each = 3000 tonnes

Production and export

Conceptual estimate 3600 tonnes

Separation	30%	1080 tonnes	(25–35%)
Compression and export	30%	1080	(25–35%)
LNG and refrigeration	40%	1440	(38–44%)
	Total	3600 tonnes	

Utilities

Conceptual estimate 1200 tonnes

Construction facility	90%	1080 tonnes
Workshop and laboratory	10%	120
	Total	1200 tonnes

Power generation

Conceptual estimate 1800 tonnes

Generators and switch gear	88%	1584 tonnes	(85–90%)
Turbo exhaust	12%	216	(+ or –1%)

Accommodation

Conceptual estimate 2500 tonnes

Upper and lower living quarters	2500 tonnes

This assumes one single lift which, due to other considerations could become two lifts, probably split 45%/55%.

The production of the feasibility estimate would follow the same path as the conceptual estimate, drawing on existing data to generate the planning and cost figures. One major difference would be that the risk and associated contingency elements would be defined. One element of that would be anticipated growth.

2.6   Growth factors

One of the major reasons for overruns of time and resources is what is termed 'growth', and there are many factors which contribute to the increase in work scope. These would include:

- Design errors
- Design changes
- Field changes
- Damage
- Underestimation
- Bad management
- Regulation changes
- Incomplete work
- Rectification
- Material delays

These are only a few of the causes; there are of course many more. To a large extent they can be quantified and therefore anticipated.

In our statistics, if we have taken the total cost and man-hours actually required to do the work, all additions to the net scope are covered. We have an average global result and in theory, if our project runs no better or worse than average, we should have no problem. This may constitute a problem or at least, generate a searching question when the contractor's bid is received for the work and it is 30+% under your estimate!

The contractor will bid only on the scope presented, and rightly so; it is not the contractor's prerogative to add anticipated growth to the bid. The contractor is in a very competitive market and is using a very sharp pencil, as they say, to make the best bid possible. His knowledge of potential growth will be very good, if not excellent, in his field of endeavour but it is not part of the scope of his first bid.

The contractor will not have allowed for growth but you must; to reduce your budget because you have a lower actual bid for the known scope is to commit a form of ritual suicide. To exercise control over the growth is one of the major tasks as is the ability to check that the scope bid, plus the anticipated growth, still remains within the project budget. To fulfil both these functions, an understanding of the source and extent of growth is required. The graph shown in Fig. 2.7 is an indication of what may be expected within construction.

One source of growth is lowered productivity. The graph Fig. 2.8 shows that, where you have a large workforce expending thousands of man-hours, productivity falls. Large workforces are difficult to supervise, problems exist in maintaining the flow of work, and for whatever reason, down time increases.

With a large workforce, there is a tendency to load manpower on to activities which may be falling behind but this in itself leads to reduced productivity, see Fig. 2.9.

Increased growth can come from such things as underestimation of the man-hours required to fulfil a particular function. A job may have been estimated to take 20 hours and due to its location, as shown in Fig. 2.10, takes 40 hours, reducing the productivity by 50%.

Lack of materials is always a cause of delay, not only extending the schedule but causing workforce down time. Having the right material at the right time is essential to any project, and **good materials scheduling is not a job, it is an art.** Knowing when materials are required and their relative volume in proportion to the project duration can assist planning to schedule resources in the right proportion during the early development phases and before hard data are available, see Fig. 2.11.

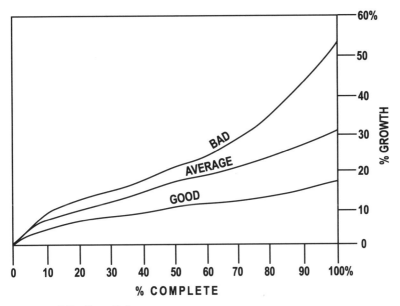

2.7   Growth in scope.

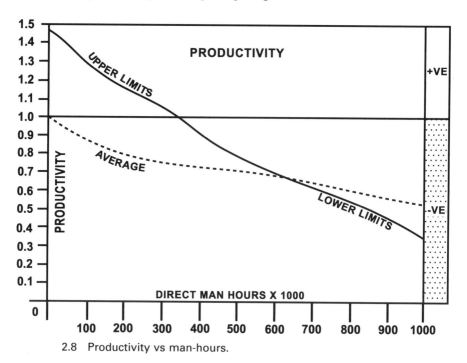

2.8   Productivity vs man-hours.

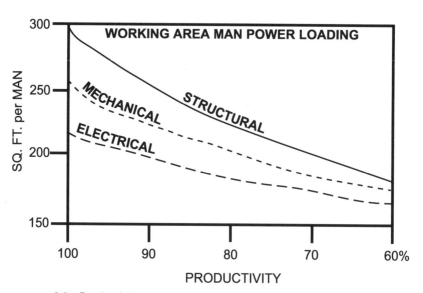

2.9   Productivity vs manpower loading.

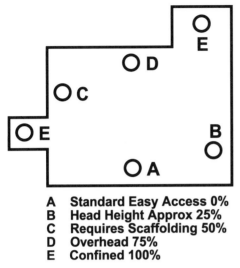

A   Standard Easy Access 0%
B   Head Height Approx 25%
C   Requires Scaffolding 50%
D   Overhead 75%
E   Confined 100%

2.10   Positional increase.

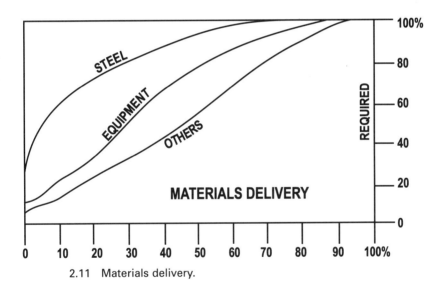

2.11   Materials delivery.

Lack of foresight is one of the major contributors to growth, the burden of which falls to a large extent on planning and supervision. Once a project is underway, the cost engineer to a large extent becomes one of the back-room boys; a very busy and important back-room boy looking after the costs, but a back-room boy nevertheless. The planning engineer on the other hand is now heavily involved in every aspect of the project both in the field and in the office.

A bad plan can create a mass of extra work if it fails to sequence the work properly and lacks foresight. The trade supervisor lacking foresight can also create the same type of problem. How often, for example, have we seen the same hole in the road opened up time and time again, or the same scaffolding taken down and put back a few days later to cope with another job by a different trade?

Using his or her own initiative, a supervisor may complete a section of work not scheduled because it is convenient at the time, only to discover later that it has to be removed for access so that some other activity can proceed. The planning engineer may sequence the work incorrectly and create the same problem.

All of these problems and those of a similar nature cause growth and this does not even take account of bad design clashes, damage, errors in general and so on. One can never overstress the role that **good planning** and **good supervision** have in maintaining **control** in its widest sense.

2.7   Applying contingency

From our initial estimates for each of the major components and using three basic scenarios, best, most likely, and worst cases can be established by applying selected 'rates'. This is a simple computer function and allows limits to be controlled, i.e. the worst and best elements limited to an under- or overrun probability of say 10 or 12.5%. The computer input is derived as shown on the contingency application flowsheet, Fig. 2.12. The results of the scenarios are then processed using a selected simulation – Monte Carlo is one of the most favoured.

From the simulation a cumulative probability curve would be generated. From the cumulative curve shown in Fig. 2.13, using selected percentages, the total allowable budgets can be defined in terms of where they intercept the baseline estimate figure.

Common entry percentages
Company overrun allowance   80%
Project manager's budget   65%
50/50 estimate   50%
Most likely   25%

The difference in budget cost between the most likely and the 50/50 estimate is the project contingency. The establishment of these two parameters will require a redistribution of cost to effect detailed budgeting.

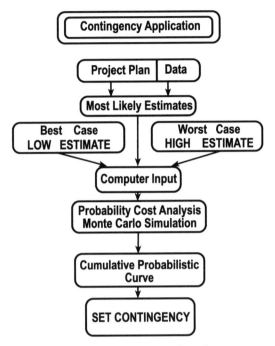

2.12   Contingency application flowsheet.

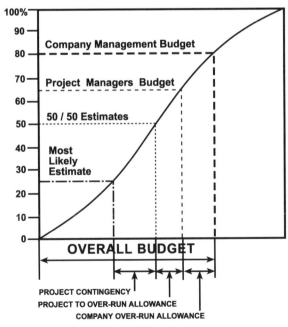

2.13   Cumulative probability curve.

Within the feasibility phase, the budget figures obtained would be for information only. Should the project receive the go-ahead and move forward to the development phase, this exercise, based on further levels of information and detailed analysis, would be used to set the budget levels.

3
Contract plan

3.1 Control starts

As a project moves towards the development phase the contracts section or department must start preparing for the award of contracts, and that requires a plan of action to be developed. Where the work will be performed and to which contractor a contract is awarded can have the greatest influence on the control that the company has on the final outcome of the project. It is therefore not something which can be approached lightly, or without an in-depth study of the elements which will or might have a bearing on the final contract.

Control starts by ensuring that all elements relating to the awarding of a contract have been considered, covering all the key phases from an initial project plan through to pre-mobilisation of the contractor.

3.2 Contract action checklists

No action checklist can pretend to be complete – companies and contracts are too diverse in their internal strategies and products. What is presented is a broad guideline which will place the reader on the right track, and to anyone new to contracts, or for use as a project manager's checklist, what follows will form an invaluable contract tool.

Project phase

The project phase identifies which resources and general information will be required if and when a contract team needs to be mobilised.

- Identify the contract required activities
- Plan the contract preparation and work timing
- Resource the contract preparation
- Prepare a budget for the work
- Establish a contract policy and strategy
- Prepare systems and procedures contracts

- Examine financial influences, phasing, taxation, grants, etc.
- Verify the team's working area, equipment, support resources

General considerations

- Need for approval by tender board (authorised signatory related to contract value)
- Government agencies' consultation
- Partner consultation
- Review bodies
- Materials purchasing arrangements and approvals

Prepare a contract schedule

To be able to set contract award dates, the contracts section needs to examine its work load and allocate time and resources accordingly, in order to:

- Define the scope of the work
- Define the overall work schedule
- Establish the budget availability and phasing
- Contract staff resources
- Generally define interfaces with other departments by consulting:
  - Planning
  - Cost engineering
  - Design
  - Engineering
  - Construction
  - Other projects
  - Other contracts
  - Senior management
  - Legal
- Perform contractor initial screening
- Establish tender evaluation criteria and principal evaluation panel

Contractor selection phase

An important part of a contract department's responsibility is the selection of suitable contractors who have the ability to bid for the work. The costs expended by a contractor in preparing a tender document for a major contract are such that no contractor should be requested to tender who does not have a fair chance of obtaining the work. You now have to:

- Consult contractor appraisal information
- Prepare a broad list of suitable contractors

- Screen and prepare an initial shortlist
- Assess the shortlist
- Finalise the list of contractors to tender, based on:
  – Capability and capacity to do the work
  – Suitability
  – Financial stability
  – Industrial relations stability and safety record

Contract document phase

- Prepare conditions of contract
- Define scope of work to be undertaken
- Draw up technical specifications and related drawings
- Define co-ordination procedures, control mechanisms, and planning and progress control systems
- Prepare specifications and pricing schedules
- Identify tender document requirements
- Establish what contract type will be required

General considerations

- Maintenance and defect liability
- Insurance indemnity
- Guarantees and warranties
- Secrecy agreements
- Control dates, i.e. start, completion, milestones
- Patents
- Payment periods
- Escalation
- Audit requirements
- Employer representatives
- Grants
- Taxation
- Material purchase controls
- Local content
- Currency
- Progress measurement
- Quality assessment and quality control
- Risk/possible liabilities/insurance

Pre-tender phase

- Finalise tender plan
- Finalise tender documents

- Obtain approval of plan and tender
- Finalise tender invitations

Tender and evaluation phase

The maintaining of clear concise records during this phase is essential, as once the evaluation phase is complete the tender board must be appraised of what has transpired.

- Finalise review panel membership
- Issue tender security document
- Control tender receipt and opening
- Apply evaluation criteria
- Deviations and qualification record
- Price, delivery, location, logistics, quality, performance
- Financial cover obtained
- Clarifications required
- Contractors' control ability

Tender board recommendation phase

On completion of the evaluation, the recommendations will be placed before a tender review board for them to make the final selection. The board will consider the analysis conducted and the recommendations from a different standpoint – that of the company and investor. Their judgement will have to include external influences which may be financial, governmental, political or whatever.

Evaluation

- Financial
- Technical
- Programme
- Managerial/IR/safety
- Sensitivities
- Considered elimination

Financial

- Financial cover statement
- Estimated overall contract value
- Analysis of estimate vs financial statement
- Assessment of contract review limit
- Contingencies/escalation

Operation

- Maintenance
- Standardisation
- Spares
- Government considerations
- Partner comments
- Number and type of associated subcontracts
- Material and equipment requirements
- Location and logistics

Pre-mobilisation

Once a contract has been awarded, and prior to work commencing, a short period of time exists during which the ground rules can be established for company interfacing and communication/reporting requirements. This is also the time to ensure that the contractor has the same understanding of the elements of the contract as was intended. You may be taking on board a contractor's system. Do you, or more importantly, do the people who will have to work with it really understand it?

Requirement considerations

- Reports
- Payments/currency
- Measurement/costs/evaluation
- Progress/physical status/financial
- Escalation
- Resources/man-hours
- Certification
- Variations
- Claim handling
- Stoppages
- Contract extensions

3.3   Contract type vs project knowledge

The goal aimed for by all management is to put out for tender a fully-defined and designed project requirement. Unfortunately, that is seldom if ever achieved. Where the project consists of a number of major elements and development phases, the stage of definition will be different for each. In each case the type of contract from one unit or phase to the other would differ. Figure 3.1 gives an indication of the possible contract variability,

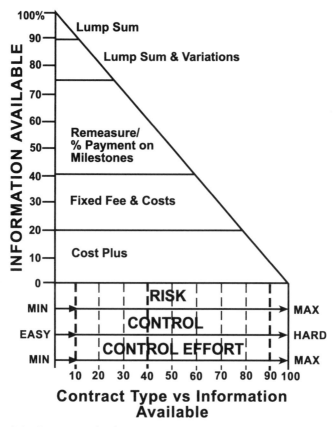

3.1   Contract selection.

based on the project information available at the time of tender. In simple terms, the less defined the project, the greater the risk; the less control we have, the more lenient the contract type needs to be.

It is therefore obvious that there will come a time, with some contract awards, when some deep soul searching will be required as to whether to place the contract now or to delay. It is in these situations where risk analysis and schedule pressure will dominate the equation.

3.4   Progress problem

A problem which often occurs when progressing an activity is what percentage to allow for a part complete item, or what to allow at a specific stage of completion of an item. Where the item has the ability to be measured easily the problem does not arise. If on the other hand we follow the drawings produced by a design contractor, progressing the work can present

PROGRESS OF DRAWINGS

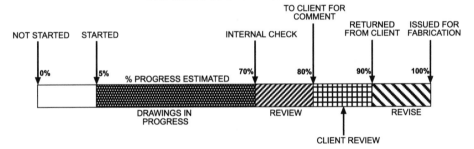

3.2   Drawing progress percentages.

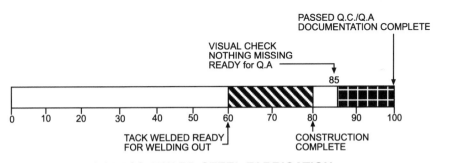

PROGRESS AWARD STEEL FABRICATION

3.3   Typical fabrication milestones.

problems because a completed drawing may be totally rejected and therefore has no real value. On the other hand, it would be unfair for a design contractor to wait until a drawing was fully approved before any payment was made. To overcome such a problem a method of assessing progress on such items needs to form part of the contract documentation.

The same sort of thing can apply even to steel fabrications. It would be an inaccurate measure of progress if all items were to wait until they were fully welded out before they could be progressed. Under-measurement of progress is just as bad as over-measurement since schedule-related decisions would be inaccurate and actions may be taken that could have been avoided.

Figures 3.2 and 3.3 show practical examples that set percentages for various stages of completion.

3.5   Interrelationships

The contract elements that are being defined indicate the desirability for a deeper understanding of the need for efficient departmental and company interrelationships. Interrelationships in this sense relate to the project functions and how they relate to the project as a whole, to the management of the project and to the relationship between groups especially with regard to information flow.

To be efficient, an understanding of project functions is essential. You may consider that within your sphere of activity you are working well and doing a good job but this may not be the case. Far too often we see discipline experts who are function foolish. As an example, we may see an outstanding, legally astute contract which nevertheless lacks the key elements required for progress control or the monitoring needed for planning and costing. On the other hand, we may see a technically brilliant schedule which fails to consider the limited on-site storage available to the materials group.

There are problems of this nature within every discipline, caused in the main by having too concentrated a focus on one's own discipline and a lack of understanding of the essential needs of others. A concentrated discipline focus may earn the engineer a number of Brownie points but will not assist the manager who must maintain efficient interrelationships.

4.1   Work scope definition

The component of any project is the work that has to be done. A success-ful project is one where the work is completed on time, within the budget, and to the standard required. To achieve these goals, we first need to know exactly what work has to be done. Once we know what has to be done we can establish the cost, the resources, the materials and a logical method of completing the work, see Fig. 4.1.

One of the first uses of the work scope is in the preparation of the logic networks, the gross work scope being broken down into suitable activities contained within the network structure. To do this successfully it is neces-sary to have a written form of the scope per activity. By defining the scope we are able to establish, with a higher degree of accuracy, the duration, resources and cost of an activity. By defining the scope in relationship to the network, it must also conform to the network tiering system.

Tiering and aggregation

The tiered structure not only provides a better understanding of the project as a whole and how each activity contributes to the project entity but also accomplishes activity aggregation. To facilitate this aggregation a minimum of three levels of work scope definition are required, see Fig. 4.2.

- Level I   General Instruction
- Level II   Scope Definition
- Level III   Task Sheets

Level I   General Instruction (GI)

GIs relate directly to the activities contained in the master network and define in written terms what the activity is designed to cover but avoid the small detail. In my experience this is a document every manager makes full use of.

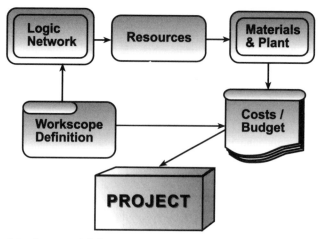

4.1   Cost establishment.

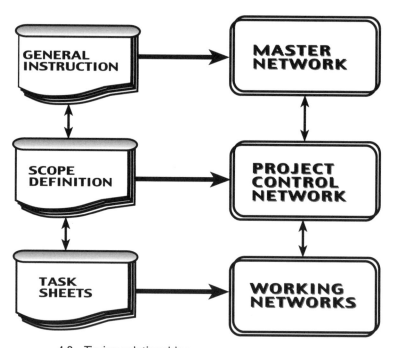

4.2   Tiering relationships.

Level II   Scope Definition (SD)

The scope definition relates to the project control network activities and provides an overall starting point for the work. The General Instruction (GI) originates from the scope definition aggregation. From the scope definition, the work can be split into its various sub-elements e.g. the task sheet.

Level III   Task Sheets

Task sheets are discipline-oriented and define in more detail the work required to be done by a specific discipline. As such, they are designed to identify the work to individual discipline managers and supervisors.

Typical example of man-hour breakdown

A simplified example of the breakdown using hours only is as follows:

Level I   General Instruction
Construct module 'X' 250000 hrs

Level II   Scope Definition
Construct module X [discipline breakdown]

Structure	100000 hrs
Mechanics	60000 hrs
Electrics	40000 hrs
[Piping]	50000 hrs
Total	250000 hrs

Level III   Task Sheets
Construct module X
Piping [fabricate and install]

System		
	A	10000 hrs
	B	20000 hrs
	C	5000 hrs
	D	15000 hrs
	Total	50000 hrs

The foregoing example explains the basic principle. In practice a GI would be made up from a number of scope definitions and a vast amount of detail as indicated in the typical contents.

Typical contents

In general terms all three documents would contain similar information, but related to its specific level of detail:

- Individual sheet number
- General heading
- Specific heading

- Assignment code number
- Definition of the scope
- Man-hours per discipline
- Cost per discipline and others
- List of drawings
- Specifications
- Special requirements
- Network activity reference
- Target start and completion dates
- Duration
- Percentage complete

The format may vary slightly from project to project to meet the specific project requirements or to accommodate the project software. To access this type of information through a computer network system is an invaluable tool for company management.

Non-network activities

Where an activity is not shown on the network, but needs to be costed, e.g. management, service function, or where inclusion in an activity would be misleading, a cost element sheet should be raised and monitored individually.

Project master file

The master file is a permanent record of planning and cost operation. Master files would contain all SDs and be maintained in book and disk form, segregated by GI. The master file forms a major information source for building a company historical data bank, updating company norms, developing graphical estimating curves, establishing contingency factors and so on. Ideally the information derived would be placed in a computer based data bank for ease of access, and for the formation of a computerised estimating programme.

It is advisable that at least one copy in book and disk form be held in a safe location, not in the same building as the other master files. Copies should be clearly marked 'Master File'. It is advisable that the master file be updated once per month, normally at the completion of each monthly report.

Schedule updating of SDs

Reporting progress to management requires the selection of the most appropriate level of detail. Too much detail only leads to a swamping of

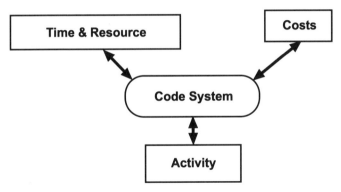

4.3   Integration of project control elements.

information, too high a level and key areas of concern become hidden through absorption. Calculation of progress using the SDs as the vehicle for assessment will present the right level of detail and result in a more than sufficient degree of accurate progress reporting and forecasting. Developing a suitable coded structure is a highly individual thing. What would suit one company would not suit another. Many of the project management software programs offer a ready-made coding structure with automatic aggregation. The software coding systems allow a code structure to be developed, linked through common codes which bring together all the key project control elements for integrated analysis, see Fig. 4.3.

What we must not do is to confuse the code structure with a company billing/invoicing code system. The code structure is for the purpose of project budgeting and control of activity costs – it is a structured aggregation tool not an invoicing system.

By holding SDs data on the computer, and using various sort codes, and selections, a wealth of reports can be produced to meet all project needs. The key to the production of the relevant reports and documentation, as mentioned earlier, is in the coded structure, part of which relates to the manpower resource.

Manpower resource codes

It would appear at first sight that it should be a simple task to allocate a sort code to each trade category employed on a project. The problem lies in getting a common classification of groups and individual disciplines within the various groups.

We then have the problem of direct and indirect labour. Getting round the problem is only a matter of establishing a clear and agreed categorisation.

Direct and indirect labour

A problem often faced by a planning and cost engineer is obtaining a clear company definition of direct and indirect labour, services, management and so on. Without a clear definition as to how the various groups are to be accommodated in an estimate interpretation, errors are almost certain to occur. This can lead to over- or under-manning, or a need for resources not anticipated in both the costs and planning.

Where a resource definition does not exist, one should be established. The planning and cost engineer can then define exactly what resources are covered in any particular estimate and what has to be catered for in other ways.

In the cases where a global rate is used i.e. rate per ton/tonne (RPT), the categories of trades covered should be specified, to help in defining the groups/disciplines. A typical example for an engineering company would be as follows:

Trade groups

For the purpose of defining the split between direct and indirect labour, six groups have been identified.

Primary Trades Group I
Welder, pipefitter, plater, mechanical fitter, electrician.

Support Trades Group II
Scaffolder, rigger.

Service Trades Group III
Crane driver, storeman, grinder, labourer.

Specialised Trades Group IV
Non-destructive testing, heating and ventilating air conditioning, instrumentation, communications.

Supervision Group V
Yard superintendent, general foreman, field engineer, foreman, inspector.

Administration Group VI
Timekeeper, drawing controller, dispatcher.

The allocation of the groups will depend to a great extent on the specific project and the level of the estimate. The trade listings are not intended to cover all trades, but give a clear indication as to placement within categories.

Subcontractor trade allocation

The subcontractor, where necessary, should define his trade categories clearly using a common standard, or produce a listing of his own which conforms to his method of calculation, so that an accurate man-hour break-down can be provided for analysis.

Management

The management element is always a tricky one to estimate as it is normally treated as an add-on percentage and seldom clearly defined. This can cause problems within cost estimates when management groups are booked to projects. As a general guide, the management groups which require to be covered by the add-on percentage, and are traditionally directly involved in the project, are as follows:

Project Management Group P1
Project manager, QA manager, technical manager, construction manager, planning and cost manager.

Project Services Group P2
Planning and scheduling, cost control, contracts, administration, safety officer.

Technical Services Group P3
Project engineer, welding engineer, QA engineer, structural engineer, piping engineer, draughtsman.

Administration Group P4
Secretaries, clerks, cleaners.

Other Cost Groups P5
Costs related to plant, equipment, services, insurance, consumables, profit.

Again the foregoing is not intended to be a complete list of all trades and management types, but gives a clear indication of where various categories of trades and management should be allocated.

Typical group classification

Group	Title	Group	Title
5	General superintendent	P2	Planner/scheduler
5	Superintendent	6	Drawing controller
5	Assistant superintendent	P2	Safety officer
P3	Project engineer	P4	Administration manager
P3	Structural engineer	P4	Chief timekeeper
P3	Piping engineer	6	Timekeeper
P3	Mechanical engineer	6	Personnel/rotation officer
P3	Electrical engineer	6	Personnel/rotation clerks
P3	Instrumentation engineer	6	Dispatcher
5	Welding inspector	3	Material co-ordinator
4	NDT technician		

3	Assistant material	3	Maintenance electrician
	co-ordinator	1	Operations electrician
3	Materials	4	Instrument fitter
3	Toolroom	4	Instrument technician
3	Medic	4	HVAC
5	Catering supervisor	2	Scaffolder
3	Cook	6	Cleaner/handler
3	Steward	1	Insulator
1	Pipe/structural welder	5	Structural general
1	Electrical/steel welder		foreman
1	Structural fitter	5	Pipefitter general
1	Structural fitter electrical		foreman
1	Pipefitter	5	Welder general foreman
2	Rigger/transport	5	Rigger general foreman
3	Crane operator	5	Mechanical general
1	Mechanic		foreman
1	Millwright	5	Electrical general
1	Carpenter		foreman
2	Painter/sandblaster	5	Instrumentation general
4	LV electrician		foreman
4	HV electrician	5	Trade foreman

These are examples from a mechanical/structural engineering trades group. A civil engineering trade group would have a different list of trades. By using the foregoing example it should be easy enough to categorise almost any group.

5.1 Project functions overview

Under the heading of Project Functions many of the subjects that have been discussed will be revisited and viewed from the planning and cost manager's standpoint. In addition, subjects which relate specifically to the manager's function, organisation, and control will be defined. What follows may be termed a day-to-day working guide to all interrelationships that give a clear understanding of the essential elements. These elements form an overview of the interrelated functions within the management structure and disciplines.

5.2 Organisation

To design an effective organisation, it is essential to establish as a first priority the key project objectives, execution policies, and relationships within the company and any outside agencies. To this end, there are a number of key points which should be observed.

Key points

- Remember to allow for organisational changes that will be necessary to meet the differing requirements as the project progresses
- Establish at an early stage the extent of project team activities in relation to those of the outside contractors
- Appoint a relatively small managerial team with long term commitment
- Make decisions on organisational changes, be it in numbers of staff or responsibilities, in a timely manner
- Plan the organisation in a similar way to the rest of the project, including job descriptions and objectives
- Maintain line, rather than functional, reporting within the project team

Approach to the organisation

Key members of a project team should be appointed as early as possible. They should be expected to stay for a substantial period in order to provide continuity and leadership. The key members of the project team would be those responsible for the following functions:

- Project management
- Engineering
- Project services (contracts, planning, costs, finance, materials)
- Operations
- Administration
- Quality assurance including mechanical completion
- Safety

Flexibility of the organisation

The organisation must allow for change as the project team expands and contracts, within functions, and overall. This sets the manager the task of allowing for expansion in office space, equipment, communications, staff responsibilities, accommodation and funding. It is a case of planning ahead, how many people will be involved, what tasks they will perform, when they will be brought on board, who will supply them, what they will need with regard to space and equipment, and what has been budgeted for.

Project team job descriptions

The project team manager should prepare a job description for every member of his or her team. The process of preparing the job description assists in the detailed organisation of the workforce. In the early stages of a project, the job descriptions may need in some cases to be in 'broad brush' terms, where authorities and scope are unclear. Nevertheless, they should exist and be individually understood and agreed by the job holder.

Job descriptions should define:

- Objectives and success criteria
- Scope of work
- Lines of reporting
- Authoritative level
- Participation in meetings, reports, presentations

5.3   Levels of authority

Sufficient authority needs to be delegated within the project team so that the line manager and members of the team can respond to the majority of queries, and changes which occur within the areas of responsibility.

You may find as a manager that your authority has been limited by the project manager, which restricts your work. If your authority is limited, then your team's authority is even more restricted. Restricted limits of authority, beyond that which would be considered normal for the post, is caused in most cases either by your superior lacking confidence in your ability, or lacking confidence in his or her own ability. To be successful, the manager must have sufficient authority to meet the demands of the job. Your job description is the first check on its existence. Should it be lacking, the time to correct the deficiency is on day one and not six months into the job.

5.4   Support staff

Support staff, in the form of clerical and secretarial staff within a project team should never be underestimated, either in their numbers or in their contribution to a project. When support staff are limited, the work has to be carried out by highly paid skilled engineers, which is a total waste of money and resources. Good support staff are an asset to the project, not only in allowing the engineer or manager to devote time to that which is important but also by assisting in the task.

5.5   Project planning guidelines

The following, based on experience, is a series of guidelines which should institute a good base from which to establish a viable planning section:

Key points

- Agree objectives and constraints with all relevant parties and sections
- Base major decisions on a project model (network)
- Use sensitivity analysis to identify critical areas and concentrate efforts accordingly
- Quantify risks and make contingency plans
- Keep plans simple and ensure compatibility at different levels (I, II and III)
- Ensure that computer software systems are user-oriented and geared to project requirements

Network and data sheets

The basis for the plan should always be the project network supported by the resulting schedule. The data sheets which detail the network activities form the back-up and justification for the activity elements.

The use of the data sheets will:

- Ensure that a thorough analysis has been carried out based on the information available
- Highlight work not included in an activity which must be allowed for elsewhere
- Record all assumptions
- Form the detailed link between the plan and the costs

Project model

The project model is used to judge profitability and cash flow. It also provides a means of:

- Discriminating between alternative development schemes
- Developing project execution strategies
- Evaluating the effect of proposed changes
- Warning of future problems

An important aspect of the model is its use in risk analysis techniques. By using probabilistic analysis, fairly accurate forecasts can be made to aid policy decisions.

5.6   Use of computers

The selection of the computer system in most cases will have been performed by the company manager, probably some time in the past, and will be common on all projects. This allows the company to integrate all its projects into a company network and cost model which will be used by senior management in the making of executive decisions.

Assuming that the software is suitable for your needs there are a number of elements related to the system in general that should be checked.

- There is ample computer capacity
- There are sufficient computer units available and in good condition
- The system can be easily accessed
- There are sufficient operators who know the software in depth
- It is able to deal with multi-location feedback
- Security of information can be maintained
- A system of taking back-ups is in operation
- What other software it is compatible with (e.g. databases, spreadsheets)

As the manager you do not need to be a software expert. Knowing what it can do, so that you can make intelligent requests, is sufficient. To be knowledgeable in computers is a bonus, and a skill that no manager in today's computer-oriented world should neglect. Nowadays, we can see the steady growth of project control software and according to the claims of the software vendors, much of the current software would appear, on the surface at least, to be more than adequate for your needs. Unfortunately, that is not the case. It may meet your requirements on one project but be inadequate on another. If you are selecting a software package, think to the future.

What you do not want is to train your staff on one system and then find later that you need to start all over again some time in the future with a new one. This is not only a waste of time and money, but the expertise gained is also lost. All too often that expertise has been hard won with many long hours of operational learning, involving a few mistakes that you would not like to see repeated.

What follows, though slightly out of context with the aspect of project functions, is a natural follow-on with regard to computerisation.

Computerisation

The computer has two direct uses related to planning and several indirect uses such as databases, spreadsheets, graphics and word processing. As to the direct uses they relate to the following:

- Time and resources analysis
- Probabilistic analysis as a supplement to forecasting

5.7   Computer hardware and software systems

Over the last decade there has been an explosion in project management software. Describing them all would probably take several books and the use of that is debatable. The software you use for any particular project depends to a great extent what the company has selected as its standard system. With freedom of choice managers often select software they are familiar with which may or may not be the best for the job on hand.

With the range of what may be termed support software, the trend is now to move away from expensive 'Heavyweight packages' and use an integrated software approach, as shown in Fig. 5.1. Using the integrated approach, time and resource analysis is conducted at a high level, remaining within the limits of the software. This removes the need for major programming software.

The detailed elements related to the work breakdown structure and associated job cards are handled by the database and spreadsheet. The cost control elements are handled by the spreadsheet and/or the integrated accounts packages. The only care that needs to be taken is that the software packages are compatible and can import and export information from each other.

An example of this would be the Microsoft range of products such as:

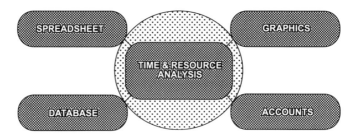

5.1   Software integration.

Project	Scheduling
Foxpro/Access	Database
Excel	Spreadsheet
PowerPoint	Graphics

In this example, the products are all from the one company but they need not be. Most of what may be termed best-seller software has a wide range of cross-compatibility. This facility allows a mix and match of many of the best software products for even better efficiency.

The advantage of this system is that the support software has many other uses within the company. The disadvantage is that if the company systems are not integratable, staff would need to be trained in their use. A few project software companies have seen the need for this type of integration and have developed fully integrated project control systems.

Now available are high-end core scheduling and resource management software packages, many of which are well known and used extensively in industry. Over the years these project management software companies have developed additional software packages, such as flexible cost managers, graphical partners for Windows with the ability to produce proposal type schedules, overview reports, document management control, and risk management using statistical simulation. Many of these systems are easy to use, and are also suitable for use on a 486 PC or better still Pentium II PC and Local Area Networks (LAN).

There are, of course, what may be termed popular heavyweight systems, such as ARTEMIS 7000 or Primavera, two of today's leaders in the power planning and scheduling field.

Typical of these software systems which designate a portable family of project management software products, is the ability to run on a variety of mini computer and workstation hardware platforms using either Digital Equipment Corporation's VMS operating system, or AT&T's UNIX operating system. In addition, they have the ability to run on IBM-compatible 486 PCs. Currently these software packages include a powerful relational database, flexible report writer with full graphics capabilities, full-screen data set editor, and user-defined windows and processes. When selecting a system, much depends on personal choice, and funds available.

5.8   Schedule control

To control the scheduling within the project there are three main areas of concern and a number of key points.

- The type/style of schedules to be employed
- The data required from contractors and its form of presentation
- Consistent and well-disciplined reporting systems

Key points

- Use networks, bar charts and milestones for schedule development
- Agree the format of schedule reports from contractors prior to contract award
- Relate payments to milestone achievement where possible to provide completion incentives
- Use simple physical measures of progress as a global check against detailed contractor reports
- Ensure that different levels of plans are compatible
- Use planned man-hours as the common progress base

Milestones

Milestones are key elements in the control process, and should be established at all levels to communicate overall project objectives. They also provide management with specific targets against which progress information can be evaluated.

Each individual project will set the 'location' of the various milestones to suit its specific requirements. Setting of milestones should reflect critical completions, sensitive target activities, and high logic dependencies. The number of milestones should never be too numerous to overstretch the contractor and act as a disincentive to complete, nor too few in order to withhold a sense of accomplishment.

Reporting mechanisms

Control depends upon the regular supply of accurate information in good time. The form of the reports and their frequency should be clearly defined within the contract. The manager should check the early reports at the start of the contract to ensure conformity; in this way reporting difficulties can be overcome before they are able to adversely affect progress control. It is well within the contractor's rights to deny his client any additional report that is not within the contract. Fortunately most contractors are flexible and prepared to produce various non-contract defined reports for the client on request. This is a favour and should be treated accordingly.

On receipt of the contractor's written reports, regular progress meetings should be set up to discuss the results. These meetings must be formal and carefully planned and structured. The minutes of the meeting should be taken by the contractor, and approved by your attendees. In this way you will be aware of the contractor's understanding of what took place. Later you may wish to bring pressure to bear on the contractor by quoting from previous minutes. The words 'and quoting from the minutes of the . . .' will have much greater impact and credibility.

5.9   Cost control guidelines

Projects may be extended in time and there is no doubt that 'time is money' or at least it costs money to maintain the resources for longer than was anticipated. This may be a difficulty but not so much of a problem if the company can sustain the cost of an overrun budget.

As the cost manager, you have a major responsibility to the company to detect any potential overrun as soon as possible and inform the management. You may disagree with the original budget at day one; if so it is your duty to express that disagreement. Cost control is not accountancy. Accountants as a general expression are in **charge** of the finances: you are in **control** of the costs. Should you lose that control for whatever reason, the project is in jeopardy and you may revert to being a highly paid bookkeeper. To prevent this possibility the following needs to be established.

- The basis of the cost estimate
- The meaning and use of project contingency
- Method of cost reporting
- Data required from contractors
- Interface with financial reporting
- Close relationship with planning

Key points

- Base the estimate on the project network, schedule and data sheets
- Use multi-value estimates to work up project budgets
- Relate project contingency to risk
- Ensure that activity responsibility is defined

- Use commitment as the key point of financial control
- Gear cost reports to forecasting trends as a catalyst for management action

Cost estimating

The main purpose of the cost estimate is to:

- Provide information on alternative options and actions as a basis for decision-making
- Establish a cost plan against which cost performance can be monitored
- Forecast cash requirements so that funds can be allocated

Activity estimate

The cost estimate is established in the main from the aggregation of the individual activity estimates. In preparing the activity estimate, the cost engineer/manager should take into account the following:

- Data from previous similar projects
- Industrial norms/man-hour standards
- Constraints imposed by the project plan
- Probable increase in the base estimate as design and development proceeds
- The anticipated market, fiscal, environmental and statutory conditions
- Estimator's personal experience
- High and low contingency values

Project contingency

The base estimate and associated probability distribution are enhanced by the addition of a project contingency. The contingency should be set at a level to cover the undefined but probable increase in the project estimate not covered by the individual activity estimates, i.e.:

- Exchange rate fluctuations
- Changes made to the execution plan
- Changes in interpretation of the project objectives
- Need to accelerate certain activities
- Major equipment damage
- Industrial action
- Major estimating, planning or construction error

This list is only an example of some of the factors which can demand additional funds. What contingency does not cover are changes to the project scope as defined in the initial project plan. Changes in scope which increase the project workload require funds to be released through a new budget allocation.

Cost reporting mechanism

The cost manager will be required to produce a variety of reports to meet the managerial requirements. Some of these reports will be limited in detail, others very well detailed. As a basic requirement all should contain the following:

- Original budget estimate
- Current control estimate (authorised funds)
- Commitment
- Expenditure status
- Forecast to completion
- Commitment on variances

5.10   Finance and administration

Finance and administration are not strictly part of the cost manager's role but are closely linked functions. As a project services manager, finance and administration is often, though not always, a part of the manager's responsibility. As a guide to the manager, there are a number of actions that should be taken, and facts established, i.e.:

- A firm budget figure for the project
- Procedures for approvals and payments to contractors
- Common methods of communication
- Personnel policies
- Procedures with regards to housekeeping, e.g. filing, petty cash, typing services

Key points

- Agree and publicise precise definitions of key project terms, e.g. budget, contingency, commitment
- Keep accounting and cost control as separate activities
- Maintain project systems and procedures, by example and discipline from the top
- Work in conjunction with cost engineering to avoid duplication of work and effort

Project accounts

There are two distinct purposes for project accounts. These purposes are separate and in the main incompatible. As they relate to cost engineering, no attempt should be made to combine the two. The first can never be timely enough and the second can never be accurate enough to satisfy the essential requirements, which are:

1) To provide historical cost information which must be accurate and auditable.
2) To provide forward looking commitment control information which must be timely, up-to-date, and responsive to adverse trends, highlighting the action required.

Budget approval

Budget approval is given by the company on the basis of the budget submission prepared by the project manager. The important point to note is that approval of the budget does not give the project the authority to commit expenditure. It is only possible to commit expenditure when an AFE (see Chap 6) has been obtained.

Communication

The success of any project or organisation depends on the implementation of a good formal communication structure. Too often this structure is developed slowly and the project suffers the adverse effects. If no guideline is issued by the manager, staff meetings may not be conducted correctly, or may use different techniques which may lack compatibility.

As a guide to the essential features of communication, they will be considered under three main headings:

• Meetings
• Reports
• Filing

Meetings

The principal and most effective form of project communication is by face-to-face meetings between people directly involved in the running of the project. Meetings should be minuted and the minutes contain the following:

• Date and place
• Purpose of the meeting

- Those attending and their company
- Summary of major items discussed and agreed
- Allocation of responsibilities and timing of subsequent action
- Circulation

The minutes should be prepared quickly and issued as soon as possible. A common fault is the issue of minutes weeks after a meeting.

Preparation for the meeting should include:

- Circulation of the agenda
- Allocation of approximate timing of agenda items
- Advice and any relevant documentation to those attending
- Doing your 'homework' before the meeting, and preparing a list of questions to be answered

Reports

Reports may either be technical documents, providing data and comments on specific problems, equipment and the like or written statements of project status and progress. With regard to the latter, they should contain as a minimum the following:

- A statement of the original plan
- Progress made against the plan
- Deviation from the plan
- A narrative comment
- Problems encountered and anticipated
- Significant action taken
- Recommendations

Where possible, visual presentations should be made in preference to long narratives.

Filing

An effective and well-disciplined project filing system is essential on any project, both for general reference and for legal or contractual research or back-up. The filing system should satisfy the following requirements:

- All correspondence, including letters, memos and telexes
- All correspondence entered in a project file record
- Originals kept in a master file
- Action responsibility indicated on circulation copies
- Clean copy of outgoing correspondence issued to file

Keeping good files is not a simple task; it requires people who know how to run a filing system and it also requires space and storage facilities suitable for the task. Being able to access a specific letter or other document may save the company a great deal of money, and in any case it is a legal requirement to maintain project records.

5.11 Contracting

With regards to the contractor or subcontractor the manager should establish:

- The role of the contractor
- The form of contract
- Evaluation and selection procedures
- Control mechanisms

Key points

- Develop a plan for the contracting activities
- Use competitive bid lump sum contracts whenever possible
- Do not insist on lump sum contracts if this implies very large risks for the contractor or if lump sum is unlikely to be achieved in practice
- Include within all contracts a comprehensive means of agreeing the time and cost consequences of change
- Use standard procedures as the basis for bid evaluation and incorporate a balanced assessment of engineering management and commercial proposals
- Use a company standard form of contract where possible
- Agree contract control mechanisms with the contractor before recommending award of the contract and include this within the contract document
- Do not try to commit the contractor to unrealistic deadlines
- Invite bids from authorised contractors who have been subject to a prequalification assessment

The contractor's role

Consider carefully why the contractor is being used, i.e. what is being paid for – men, expertise, systems, management, facilities. It is important that the appropriate roles and relationships are established between the company and the contractor at the outset. The company's aim must be to complement and not duplicate the contractor's efforts and to **manage the contract not the contractor**. Far too often the reverse is true with the client becoming no more than additional project supervision. The company's main role is to assist by giving additional technical information, management and process help.

Contract types

No matter what type of contract is used it should be competitively bid. The objective should be to maximise the incentive for the contractor to perform by relating his profit to his performance.

The most common types of contract are:

- Lump sum, with or without adjustment
- Schedule of rates/bill of quantities
- Cost reimbursable

Lump sum

Whenever possible lump sum contracts should be used but to be able to issue a lump sum contract you require the following:

- A good definition of the work scope
- A reasonable level of risk for the contractor
- The minimum amount of potential change
- A detailed mechanism for agreeing the time and cost of changes, e.g. schedule of rates for agreed extras

These requirements imply a significant amount of project planning and definition prior to award of contract and this should not be underestimated.

Schedule of rates

This form of contract permits a degree of control over the final cost of the job without the need for precisely defining the scope of the work. It requires the following:

- Sufficient project definition to be able to provide a reasonable approximation of the scope of work and quantities involved
- Inclusion of all significant jobs within the schedule (additional materials, skills and equipment may be difficult to negotiate after contract award)
- Re-measurement of the work as it is completed
- Goodwill on both sides to agree the application of the schedule to the final work scope

Cost reimbursable

As mentioned earlier this type of contract should be avoided as historically they can lead to large overruns. There are cases where they are necessary or the risk is not significant so that this type of contract could be issued. These are:

- For design and similar services
- Where a construction contract must be let before the design is substantially complete
- Where significant changes to the scope of work can be foreseen
- When major financial risks are present which could not be sustained by the contractor

With this type of contract it must be managed and supervised very closely to ensure that the project interests are maintained. Have no fear of overmanning your control or supervision, for the associated cost of overmanning is negligible compared to the cost of an overrun.

Incentives

The aim of any incentive scheme should be to motivate the contractor's team to identify with the project objectives. Profit elements should be identified and included in the fixed part of contract payments. Payments should be made on the achievement of milestones.

Penalty clauses

Penalty clauses which may appear to be the stick related to the profit carrot are seldom of real value. They are normally not effective for many reasons, the main ones being:

- They will be reflected in the tender sum increasing project costs
- They lead to undue emphasis being placed on the contract rather than getting on with the job
- They provide the contractor's workforce with a bargaining tool
- They are seldom big enough to compensate for any loss by the company
- The workings of a normal project leave too many loopholes for the clause to be implemented

Contractor selection

In the selection of a contractor the route taken by most major companies is as follows:

- Screening of enquiries, inviting interest and specific statements of capability and resources
- An invitation to bid from a shortlist of suitable contractors
- Contract award based upon evaluation of bids in terms of technical execution and commercial proposals

Bid evaluation

Bid evaluation will normally involve independent assessment of capability. Two complementary approaches are often used:

Two stage bid

This type of approach is often reserved for major contracts. Contractors are invited to submit proposals for how, where and by whom the work would be carried out. On this basis a very limited list of contractors, numbering two or three, would be invited to participate in a detailed price bid.

Project profitability evaluation

An assessment is made of the effect on ultimate project profitability by using one contractor as opposed to another. The assessment uses a project model and project team judgement on the key factors affecting the outcome of the contractor's performance. In this way the skills and shortcomings are quantified in financial terms and compared with the price quoted for the work.

In the simplest of terms, they may be cheaper but take longer, they may be more expensive but quicker. If an oil field comes on stream or a process plant is completed earlier than planned, it could show additional profit overall. On the other hand, there may arise a problem not previously identified, i.e. which one of the contractors has the ability to cope much better than another.

The decision must also take into account several factors which cannot be directly assessed in terms of profitability, such as:

- Governmental requirements and pressures
- Company overall contracting strategy, i.e. spread of work amongst available contractors to maintain a future resource or simply to parallel the work.

Contracts committee

The instigation of a contracts committee is standard practice in almost all large companies. They are there to police the action of the tender board to ensure adherence to proper procedure, and to view the actions and recommendations of the tender board to ensure that they are in the best interests of the company as a whole. The tender board's function is to evaluate the various tender submissions and make their recommendations to the contracts committee.

The contracts committee will approve:

- The contractor shortlist
- The award of contracts above certain financial levels
- Changes of contracts above certain financial levels
- Negotiated contracts

5.12 Design management

Design contracts and the final product are one of the most difficult phases to manage. It is during this phase that the company can exercise its greatest control on the final outcome of the project. A good design well conceived is a major project asset; a bad design is a disaster. Managing a design contractor needs experience, not technical experience as one might think, as that can be called in as required. Organisational ability is the prime quality required to manage this type of contract, and ideally the manager would be technically competent and a first-class organiser.

Key points

- Establish an integrated design team. Engineers should co-operate with the contractor's staff rather than act in a purely supervisory role
- Establish a clear distinction between conceptual and detail design
- Identify long lead items as an early priority
- Establish a detailed plan and get commitment to it
- Complete design before award of fabrication contracts
- Allow a realistic time for design evolution and do not try to economise on resources
- Carefully plan the interfaces between design and procurement, especially in relation to vendor information, which is always a problem
- Ensure that construction and commissioning considerations are incorporated in the design and design documentation from the outset
- Apply quality assurance procedures from the outset
- Ensure that adequate weight-control engineers are employed who will make an effort to control weight not just monitor it. Every engineer must be weight-control minded
- Plan the work from the construction phase working back to the design phase to establish ROS (required on site) dates to set design completion requirements

The design team

The objectives of the design team may be stated simply.

- To produce a design which optimises project objectives in terms of technology, cost, quality and time

- To complete sections of the design before letting corresponding construction contracts
- To minimise changes once construction starts

Setting up a successful team depends on personalities as well as systems. A good design requires a high degree of concentrated effort and is more likely to be achieved if:

- The team is well led
- The team has clearly defined objectives
- The team is in one location and separate from the parent organisations
- The team is largely self-contained
- Senior team members are committed to success
- The project runs to an established and agreed schedule
- Company and contract staff work together on problems

Procurement related to design

Equipment procurement must be closely linked with the design programme through the ROS dates to ensure the timely delivery of the equipment and related vendor information. A schedule for the supply of vendor information should form part of the contract document with the supplier.

Should a separate group be used for procurement, careful attention should be paid to the setting up and monitoring of the systems and mechanisms as follows:

- Preparing tender documents
- Answering queries
- Receiving bids
- Bid review
- Supplier selection
- Expediting
- Supply of vendor data

Change control

Changes within a project are one of the most time consuming and costly things which can happen to a project. If they are extensive or affect a critical area, they can be severely disruptive to both the schedule and the budget. It is therefore the responsibility of the manager to see that clearly defined control procedures are implemented. To be able to do this the manager must establish:

- A clear statement of the base from which the claim will be made
- Effective procedures for the preparation, evaluation, and approval of changes
- Discipline within the project to ensure compliance with set procedures

Key points

- Change control procedures must be simple and understood by all team members. They must allow for prompt response and approval by authorised personnel
- The procedure must be flexible and allow for changing emphasis depending on the project phase
- Change in documentation should not be allowed to follow approval. An analysis of the consequences on cost, time and quality must accompany the request for change
- Where changes relate to contractual terms and conditions, the time and cost implications must be agreed and signed by the contractor prior to the change approval
- Change procedures should be incorporated in all contracts detailing the basis for assessment of cost and time effects and binding the contractor to implement with minimum impact
- The later a change is introduced the greater is the impact on cost and schedule
- Minimise the amount of change by allocating sufficient time and resources to the preparation and planning of the key aspects of the project
- Ensure that no opportunity to improve project profitability is missed and only clearly beneficial changes are implemented
- Changes which relate to safety must be given full consideration

The most significant decisions about the project are made at the conceptual design stage of project definition. It is appropriate at this time to conduct the first full design quality assurance audit during the final stages of conceptual design and before the recommendations are approved.

The main aim is to put forward the best design prospect possible to the detailed design group, making their work easier, and the final design better. Improvements to the design, changes to regulations, and human error cannot be avoided and therefore changes are inevitable.

5.13   Materials and procurement

During the design phase the materials management and procurement section is presented with a number of major tasks: selecting vendors/suppliers for all the equipment, bulk materials, fittings; obtaining vendor data required by the design team; expediting information and materials; logistics. To function properly procurement staff must be well organised and disciplined and well supported by the company in their actions.

The following are a number of key points:

- Appoint a procurement manager within the project team
- Establish a bidders and vendors list with due consideration of past records

- Ensure that contractors have effective materials control procedures and staff of an adequate calibre to support them
- Establish detailed guidelines on documentation from the supplier to ensure it is adequate for certification consistent with company requirements
- Ensure close liaison and co-operation between materials management and quality assurance within the team
- Ensure the company has access to secondary suppliers who are effectively controlled through their 'main' contractor

Project team responsibilities – procurement

The procurement manager's responsibility is to get the right material to the right place at the right time. A simple statement which involves:

- Establishing a materials plan and estimate of the manpower required
- Vetting of contractors who may be able to undertake procurement of materials
- Control of procurement activities during the life of the project
- Creation of a team to undertake the procurement tasks
- Liaison with all other groups concerned with materials

A member of the materials team should be permanently based at the office or site of every major contractor with responsibility for all materials at that location. The team member will be the contact for all material questions for both the company and the contractor and also oversee the safe handling and storage of materials.

Monitoring procurement

As with every other discipline, procurement requires to be progressed. Regular progress reports should include:

- Activity percentage progress
- Out-to-bid items
- Contracts awarded (purchase orders placed)
- Compliance with required-on-site dates

The terms and conditions of purchase orders should be checked so that they comply with the following:

- Technical specification
- Certification
- Testing, commissioning and acceptance including extended warranties
- Payment
- Warranties and delivery guarantees

- Preservation, storage and transport
- Access to suppliers and secondary suppliers
- Documentation
- Shipping and customs control
- Any other local import regulations

Suppliers

The purchase order terms and process of vendors should ensure that:

- Materials and equipment are produced to a predetermined schedule
- Progress against the schedule is regularly reported
- Project team representatives (QA) can check the progress being made and production processes being used both in the supplier's works and in the works of any secondary supplier
- Materials are clearly marked, preserved and securely stored until delivery

Site control

Adequate provision should be made in all fabrication and erection contracts to ensure that materials are properly received, stored and issued. The contractor's internal control procedures should be reviewed before contract award and monitored during execution.

The winding up of materials on-site should be considered at an early stage, in particular the method of control, identification, and disposal of surplus materials.

5.14 Quality assurance

Quality assurance is applied to the design, procurement, construction, commissioning, operation and maintenance of all structures and systems which are vital to the safety and availability of any installation. To this end it is necessary to establish:

- The quality requirements and objectives of the project
- The scope of activities to be undertaken in order to achieve the objectives

Key points

- The project quality plan must be developed as an integral part of the overall project plan
- Set up effective procedures to minimise abortive work as early as possible, e.g. interfaces, weight, process, change control

- Involve the certifying authority for the project from the beginning
- Development, surveillance and evaluation of the project quality assurance programme
- Control the project engineering dossier, including expediting, receipt, review, storage, distribution and division of documents
- Ensure that superseded documents are withdrawn
- Liaison with the certifying authorities, ensuring that all necessary certification activities are integrated into the overall project plan
- Take an active roll in the development and control of the mechanical completion procedures and implementation

Conclusion

For the overall project control to ensure project success, it is essential that good planning and scheduling operations are in place. Project success is in itself directly related to the setting of realistic objectives controlled by efficient systems, which are **accepted and utilised at all management levels**.

These simple facts are never more apparent than when you are seconded to a project which is overrunning both schedule and budget, and requires prompt corrective action to be taken. There are of course occasions when the whole project has been underestimated, and all you can hope to do is lessen the impact. In most cases the project has lost the control and direction necessary to achieve its goals. It is in situations like these that good planning and cost control has the ability to turn things around.

But it must be emphasised that systems and methods will not do it on their own. They need good people to operate and 'sell' them, often to disillusioned management. And let us not forget the old saying which is true of all computerised systems – 'garbage in, garbage out' – which brings us back to people!

We read in the papers of a nuclear submarine base which has just had a cost overrun of some £800 million. Was it because of the planning and cost control systems, or was it the people who managed, planned and costed the project who failed in their duties?

The sophisticated software systems in operation today have major advantages over what existed less than a decade ago but they do have one practical disadvantage. If its full potential is to be realised, today's software requires a good planning technician who is able to get to know the system in depth. Efficiency of output analysis within the system, with regard to progress, logic changes, resource and duration modifications, additions and subtractions of work, breakdown and the like become a full-time occupation.

When this duty falls on the planning engineer, less and less of his or her time is spent in the field. Only by constantly viewing the work, making progress checks, talking to engineers, supervisors and tradespeople can the planning engineer keep up to date with the latest manufacturing/construction techniques. Such field knowledge is a major advantage when plans/schedules are being devised, updated or modified.

With regard to computer systems a working knowledge of the particular software in use allows the engineer to ask the right questions of the expert and know the answers are possible. We must never forget that in planning and cost control, the computer and its software are only tools – very good tools but still tools – and must be used wisely and judiciously. This brings us back again to people, and it is the planning and cost manager's responsibility to ensure that resources are managed in a professional manner.

6

Project programming and support information

6.1 Project start

With the advancement of the conceptual phase the project starts to take shape. Project teams are selected starting with the discipline leaders/ managers, and the manager's first task is to draft an organogram for the tasks to be undertaken by his or her team. Members of the team may be drawn from various backgrounds, ongoing projects, head office, contract personnel and new hires and this mixture of staff brings with it a breadth of experience and understanding which is a definite plus. On the negative side is the diversity of working methods, which can lead to conflict and lack of integration.

The manager must set a common standard, covering methods of working, and also performance expectations. The words the manager does not want to hear are 'I did what I did on the last job and thought it would be okay'. It may have been okay on the last job but is entirely wrong for this one. To ensure this does not happen, the manager must make sure there is a guideline for the staff to work to.

Detailed project procedures may take some time to produce and not be available immediately but a general overview/philosophy of the function in written form should be available from day one. To the skilled engineer, the document will establish the method the manager intends to adopt. To the more junior members, it will not only establish the method but will accelerate their climb up through the learning curve.

In preparing the document, it is necessary to start in the simplest way, remembering that it may be read for approval by someone who may be excellent in their own field but have a limited understanding of yours. A project services manager, for example, may have come to the post from engineering, accounts or contracts but still could be in the position of having to approve your document. If this is the case, the positive spin-off is that the more someone understands your discipline, the more able they will be to give assistance should it be required.

Part of that understanding is being aware of many of the terms used which, if not defined, can lead to confusion and misunderstanding. We tend to use the words 'schedule' and 'programme' freely – often they appear to be referring to the same thing – and in general conversation this is acceptable. They are of course not the same, referring to similar, but different information. To avoid confusion it is advisable to define what is meant by the following.

The schedule

The schedule is a document with the primary function of presenting dates and durations in graphical or tabular form.

The programme

A programme not only indicates dates and durations, but includes logical sequencing, resources, and other relevant information. The information may be contained within one document, or many, and the sum of that information is the programme.

Computer program

Relates to the software used to process the data.

Control programme

The control programme is a collective term which relates to all the information elements necessary to effectively control the targets that have been set. The control programme is the vehicle to communicate all the essential information items such as:

- Defining the work to be done, in detail or 'broad brush' terms
- Forecasting start and completion dates
- Identifying critical and sub-critical items
- Providing a visual means of communication and comment, for better programme definition
- Providing a performance yardstick
- Acting as a base for preparing cost estimates
- Assisting people to think logically as to how they will execute the work

6.2   Preparing the schedule or network

Preparing the schedule is the starting point in project control as, for the first time, ideas take on the mantle of reality and possibility. The schedule starts to answer all the 'when?' questions – when can we start?, when will we need delivery?, when will it be complete? and so on. It also starts to answer the 'who?' and 'how many?' questions as resource information is added. As the logic starts to firm up, it then has the ability to answer the 'how?' questions, by sequencing the work.

Good plans/schedules do not happen by accident, they are only achieved through hard work. **A first class schedule may appear the work of a genius, but there is no doubt that genius in this case is 1% inspiration and 99% perspiration.**

The planning engineer must ensure that he/she has made every effort to gather all relevant information, from whatever source. The information available will vary in detail depending on the phase of the proposal or project, and therefore seeking information will be a constant task. In the establishment of durations, resources and logical sequencing, use should be made of historical data, and also communication with other engineering, commercial, and administration departments, where assistance may be given.

Initially a rough draft should be prepared, covering all key activities, and reviewed for compliance with the company philosophy and management approval. Once agreed, the draft schedule should be prepared and issued, for use by those departments who require early guide dates i.e. contracts, procurement, recruitment, engineering and so on.

For the programme to be acceptable and viable the planning engineer must produce a programme which conforms to the concepts and philosophy of the engineering/construction group in general. To achieve this goal, it is necessary to maintain a level of formal communication through meetings and discussions. In this way casual or informal communications can be formalised and entered in the worksheet.

Communication of key information

Communication will normally take three basic forms:

- Reference drawings and sketches supplied by engineering
- Verbal communication through individual discussions and formal meetings
- The engineering method statement

Should the planning engineer find, for any reason, that there is a reluctance of the various groups to attend meetings or provide information of which they are in possession, this is the time to light the blue touchpaper, and management action should be sought. Preparing a good control programme is not only satisfying to one's ego but is fundamental to the project's viability. The planning engineer must also ensure that the various groups have been supplied with the information they require. The necessity for the free cross-flow of information at this time cannot be emphasised too strongly.

Engineering method statement

The engineering method statement is a key document in the production of a reliable programme. It enables the planning engineer to establish the preferred order of development and construction. The detail contained within the statement will depend largely on how advanced the project is, at the time of preparing the statement. This in turn will be reflected in the quality of information presented in the programme.

The method statement is intended to supplement any design drawings which are available and should be completed as far as knowledge allows. Ideally the method statement should be presented to the planning department before planning begins. Under normal circumstances, the planning engineer will be required to expedite the detailed activity information, and the contents of the method statement should be used as a checklist to assist in this task.

The method statement is a complex and fairly comprehensive document and should contain, but not be limited to, details of the following:

- Location and project overview
- Process narrative
- Structural weights
- Equipment weights per unit
- Bulk weights or volumes per area/units
- Special package details
- Plot plans
- Flowsheets
- Overview sketches
- Contracting alternatives
- Anticipated delivery of major equipment
- Target production date, if known
- Government requirements
- Support base, if relevant
- Pipeline details, if relevant
- Anticipated contract award dates
- Anticipated national and international contracts
- Probable construction sequence of major components
- Start-up/commissioning sequence
- Areas requiring special development
- Phased or delayed completion of any system
- Pre-selected or fixed periods for major marine equipment, if relevant e.g. accommodation barge, crane barge
- Accommodation allocation restraints
- Weather conditions generally and restraints

Schedule/network review

As we have mentioned earlier, the schedule/networks need to be reviewed to establish their viability, and to do this there are various aspects which need to be considered.

- What was the basis for establishing the scope
- What historical references were used to establish durations
- Who was consulted with regard to specialised areas
- Does the sequence of events appear logical
- Do the durations appear adequate with special reference to safety, critical and sub-critical activities
- What factorisation was used, if any, for the work elements and work in other countries
- Do the milestones comply with the original philosophy and contract
- What are the major constraints in the schedule
- What is the present critical path and does it appear logical
- Is there sufficient detail in the schedule to be a meaningful control tool
- Is the schedule too detailed which makes it difficult to follow
- Will it be a simple matter to develop forecasting/trending tools
- Does the schedule have a classification
- Are there any activities where a 'guesstimate' has had to be made due to adequate detail not being available

Project plan – what is it?

The project plan is the key document on which the company will base its estimate for the potential project or tender submission, as the case may be. It will form part of the contract documentation if the work is obtained and will be a yardstick in assessing the company's performance. The document will 'spell out' in graphical and written form how the plan was developed and how it will be managed. It will include notes on software and hardware to be used and be backed by the planning procedures. It must clearly demonstrate that the techniques used in establishing the plan, and within the project, conform to good planning practice.

The vehicle for demonstrating those techniques and their proper application is the project planning procedure which should cover all aspects of project planning. In the early phase of a project there may be no project planning procedure available, in which case, the company procedure would be referenced. Each project has its own characteristics and it is, therefore, anticipated that there would be minor differences between the company guidelines and the working procedure, to achieve the same goals.

Project plan viability

The company management and/or client must be convinced that the 'schedule' and its sundry components are logical, practical and achievable, and that the resources are adequate to meet programme requirements. To demonstrate this point, the planning engineer should make a clear reference to existing historical data, and clearly state all assumptions that have had to be made because of a lack of information or for whatever other reason.

To ensure that the schedule has the necessary commitment to make it workable, agreement needs to be obtained from each project section, i.e.: engineering, procurement, construction, cost, management and so on. This can only be achieved by demonstrating the schedule's viability and by taking advice and making amendments, where necessary.

Subcontractors' schedules

No major project today is undertaken without the use of subcontractors and therefore the validity of all subcontractor schedules must also be assessed. To be able to do this effectively, it is advisable to produce an in-house key activity programme. The programme can then be used to check the main activities by comparing it against the schedule/programme submitted by the contractor.

The contractor, with his intimate knowledge of his discipline, should in theory be more accurate and have greater definition within the activities, but you should still be able to find any major discrepancies, if they exist. To take what is offered at face value is a mistake, as anyone who has spent any time in planning will confirm; not only a mistake but often a very costly one.

The schedule developed for comparison should where possible mirror that requested from the subcontractor and include but not be limited to:

- Milestone chart
- Logic network with durations and resources
- Anticipated discipline breakdown
- Work element breakdown

Deterministic and probabilistic schedules

Once the schedule is in existence, it allows planning to conduct, as part of the routine analysis of deterministic schedules, the verification of risk and sensitivity levels. Using probabilistic analysis tools, and paying special attention to activities which have major cost and schedule impact, the risk and overall sensitivity of the schedule can be established.

6.3 Project schedules

To avoid confusion, and for the purpose of this narrative, 'schedules' will be used as a collective term for time-based networks or bar charts.

The accuracy of schedules varies greatly depending on the amount of information available. The more advanced the project, the more we know of the physical aspects of the project, the labour force performance, suppliers, equipment reliability and the like. The more information we have, the greater should be the accuracy of the schedule and therefore the fewer contingencies we need to allow in time, resources and capital.

Few large projects advance at the same pace across all major elements – a few elements may just have moved out of the conceptual phase, others may be nearing the end of design, and others under construction. This is particularly true of a phased development project, and when reviewing a schedule, it is therefore important to be aware of the stage of development on which it is based or, in other words, its classification.

By classifying the schedule, we are presented with a method of fixing, within certain limits, the element of risk in meeting the schedule criteria. The lower the classification, the greater the contingency which must be allowed in the prediction of dates, duration and resources. There are three basic classifications covering the main phases of almost any project.

C   Pre-project
B   Detail design
A   Construction and installation

These phases set the classification standards. In the early stages of a project, there are many areas unknown and untried such as design incomplete, material deliveries still to be confirmed, production rates not established. As the project nears completion, there are few surprises left and therefore the schedule and its associated documents will be more accurate.

Setting a criterion for classification allows contingency factors related to durations, resources and cost to be standardised and set at fixed controllable levels. The standardisation of these contingency factors should be developed from past project history of allowances which had to be made. A common error is to evaluate historical lack of performance and use this as a contingency factor. Historical lack of performance should only be used to alter the man-hour rates, which may be in error. In this way, improved company norms can be achieved, and better future planning and costs.

A contingency allowance on performance may be made on a new project where there are activities which are not well defined or the work is of a nature of which the company has little experience. With a fully integrated computerised system, contingency factors can be allocated to classifications which are applied automatically, either globally or to selected activities.

With tight durations, the factors can be applied to resources and to durations, **only** where the float allows. In some activities, contingencies may be applied to both resources and duration, depending on what parameters have been set for the application. Critical path activities would normally be set as resource only. Other activities with more than 20 days' float would normally be restricted to duration only. For those activities with less than 20 days' float and more than 5 days' float, a small increase in resources and/or duration may be necessary.

6.4   Classifications

For the purposes of what follows, I have used letters to define the classifications but you could use numbers or any alpha numeric code.

Classification C – pre-project

Class C schedules are those produced up to and including the early part of detail design. They will cover all aspects of the project/contract in reasonable detail but there will be areas where information is still not available and cannot be fully quantified.

Classification B – detail design

As the design develops and the acquisition of hard data becomes available, the schedules produced will become more definitive and have a higher confidence factor although aspects of the construction may still not be clear and delivery dates would still be uncertain. Suppliers and subcontractors for much of the work would still need to be selected and delivery and completion dates established. Approvals by government bodies and other control groups would still require finalising.

Classification A – construction and installation

With the award of all major subcontracts, the schedule classification will now be designated A and would remain so to the end of the project. Very little hard data would be outstanding, and as the project progressed, a steady improvement in schedule accuracy should occur.

6.5   Information and programme tiers

To control a project which has tens of thousands of activities when taken to its lowest level, is not just difficult, it is impossible, assuming this was the only control level. If the information were presented in that sort of quantity, it would amount to a pile of paper which would only be of use as a doorstop! The secret of management and control of major projects is in the presentation of **just the right amount of information in the right form at the right time**.

To be able to communicate effectively and have sufficient information to effect control, a tiered system of schedules and associated information is required. The level of detail necessary for a client or project staff varies with their function, and the time they have available to assimilate the necessary information on which to make decisions. Making good decisions and giving direction IS management and control, and requires good communication of information.

Programme tiers

The simplest way around the problem is information tiering. Programme tiering has been with us for a number of years and is a proven and established method of working. Tiering not only allows information to be presented in a meaningful and understandable way, but also permits efficient high level processing and analysis.

The most common method of tiering is to use a basic three-level networking structure and associated documentation, as shown in Fig. 6.1, all of which integrate upwards to a project overview document normally in the form of a linked bar chart, i.e. project summary.

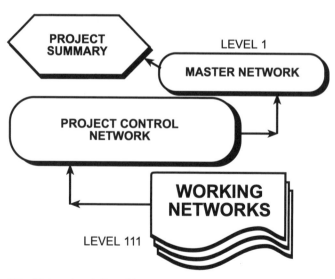

6.1   Network relationships.

- Master network – level I
- Project control network – level II
- Working network – level III

Master network – level I

The master network's function is to present an overview of the project. It is intended to communicate all the salient points and to be used as a major reporting tool to senior management. As a guide to network sizing, the activities would be in the order of 50 to 75 and also form the base for constructing the **Project Summary Bar Chart**.

Project control network – level II

The project control network is an amplification of the master network, with a ratio of approximately 3:1 or between 150 and 200 activities.

This network will be the key control network for the project and will be used not only for the closer monitoring of the physical and time elements of the project but also for the purpose of preparing cost budgets. The work breakdown structure will be derived from this level of activities.

Working networks – level III

Level III networks will cover all 'sub netting' of level II and are the detailed working level at which the work element data sheets (tracking documentation) and job carding or sheets (work allocation) will operate. Avoid at all cost any attempt to produce schedules which cover every last nut and bolt as this is a form of schedule madness that only the computer would understand and it is not good management. As the design and construction develops a large number of tracking documents will need to be produced. These documents will track such things as spool production, test packs, cubic metres of concrete, diameter inches of weld, to mention only a few.

Subcontractor networks

The subcontractor will be required to develop a similar tiered system (see planning co-ordination procedures). The top tier, level I of the subcontractor's network system, should dovetail with the project control network. This method allows various subcontractors to be integrated into the project control network, and still maintain an easily controlled network with meaningful output.

The day-to-day control of the individual subcontractor will be done at the subcontractor's detail level. The result of this monitoring will be reflected in his master network, which in turn will update the project control network.

Bar chart tiers

The bar chart is one of the more widely used formats for planning documents. It is a good graphical model for the presentation of schedule information and as such should conform to the same tiering structure employed within the network family.

Bar charts

The bar chart 'Gantt Chart' is a most effective means of schedule communication because it presents schedule information in an easily understandable format. Its advantages are numerous in communicating with all levels of supervision to provide the information they require. A simple bar chart, with only a few enhancements, can present a wealth of information to the viewer, see Fig. 6.2.

The bar chart can be enhanced by the introduction of key logic links (dummies) indicating activity dependency. Visual markers for indicating progress can use such techniques as underlining or blocking out bars and, coupled with this, 'time now', front line slippage or advancement of individual activities can be identified. Today's software allows a multitude of colour variations for indicating criticality, type of activity, and many other features.

However, in our attempts to be more sophisticated, we must avoid making the presentation too complicated. **The golden rule is to keep it simple.**

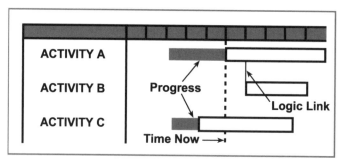

6.2   Bar chart enhancements.

6.6   Schedule support information

Preparing a schedule is a reasonably straightforward task to the trained planning engineer, provided that the information is available on which to base the schedule development. What can present a problem is the method used in achieving that development. It is therefore necessary to set objectives and define a method of working which is auditable and acceptable to management.

Dealing first with the objectives, they may be defined as follows:

- To identify the salient back-up information to be used by the planning engineer in developing the schedule/programme
- To stress the importance of maintaining an accurate record of information used

The preparation of the schedule/network requires what may be termed support information in that it justifies the durations and resources, and forms part of the back-up.

Support information falls into two primary categories:

- Schedule calculations
- Assumptions

Schedule calculation control

Schedule calculations should always be presented on a standard work sheet, the format of which may vary with the specific project or task but whose most common layout is a computer-generated spreadsheet format with column headings entered to suit specific requirements. A hard or disk copy can be taken as the actual record. Whatever method is used, the information presented should be clearly understood by others. Where necessary, notes should be added when there is a need for clarification.

Factorisation

Resource and durations are seldom used without some form of factoring to cover working environment variations. Where a difficulty factor is being used, e.g. area occupancy, restricted access, weather, the factor should be noted and, if possible, the source or reason stated in the notes.

Non-calculated durations

It is often the case that due to the lack of detail or a 'new' type of work, a best guess has to be made, based on experience. There is no fault in a best-guess estimate, as long as it is noted so that it can be revised as necessary.

Where no duration calculations are shown, but a duration has been allocated, the source if any should be noted.

Reference documents and assumptions

It may become necessary, for explanation purposes, to attach a copy of a particular reference document or to make direct reference to the particular document. In this case, notes in the estimation document should indicate that reference.

Assumptions

An essential part of any planning estimate is a listing of what assumptions have been made during the preparation of the estimate. Such assumptions assist to a large extent in defining the basis of the estimate. Should further developments clarify areas in which assumptions have been made, and a variance is required, adjustments can then be made more easily.

Minor assumptions, affecting elements within an activity, can be included in the basic calculation sheet. Assumptions which can have a major impact on the schedule should be listed separately. These assumptions, as opposed to a guesstimate, may refer to the logic, availability of major equipment, free access and so on.

The point which is being stressed is the importance of keeping good detailed records of how the durations, resources, and cost were estimated as they are important documents now and in the future.

Estimating elements

In preparing an estimate of duration or resources, there is a need to ensure that all factors are considered. To do this effectively requires the generation of a checklist which is relevant to the type of work.

The following example covers the various elements for estimating, including the data required and allowances for a typical engineering type project:

- Initial hard data/known scope
- Estimating norms
- Location work factor
- Percentage loss due to weather
- Percentage down time
- Percentage manning factor
- Percentage direct and indirect management and service companies
- Accommodation availability
- Hot working area efficiency loss

- Allowances
- Contingency

Within these 11 categories, all estimating elements can be covered. The following will explain the categories in more detail.

Initial hard data/known scope

Initial hard data covers all the known information about the project in the form of drawings, narratives etc, at the time of preparing the estimate, i.e. the base estimate.

Estimating norms

The norms are tables and historical data used for the calculation of duration and resources. They may or may not be factorised to cover location working. Should they be factorised, the base norm and the factorisation should be defined.

Location work factor

The location work factor can be simple or complex. In its simple form, it may be global in application, such as a factor of 2.5 or 3 times the base norm, covering all man-hours. It may be complex, using different factors for various systems and work locations, and may also be intended to cover various environmental conditions. The use of the factor and its components must be clearly defined to prevent 'double dipping'.

Loss due to weather

This factor is intended to cover lost time due to difficult environmental conditions which prevent work from continuing during construction. Historical weather data should be examined for the area, and an assessment made of the probable lost time. It should not be confused with that used in the location work factor which is intended to cover cold or hot weather conditions which can impact on productivity.

Down time

Down time may be defined as the inability to work due to problems arising through no fault of the workforce other than industrial action which may or may not have been instigated by the project workforce, and can be caused by:

- Lack of materials
- Plant malfunction or unavailability
- Shutdowns
- Sickness
- Industrial action
- Manpower shuttling and travel problems
- Power loss
- Special holiday periods

Manning factor

This factor is operative when manning levels are increased beyond the point where adequate working forces are available or when congestion exists, preventing clear access to work faces.

Direct, indirect and management resources

Calculations are based on direct labour (key trades). It is therefore necessary to define what indirect labour resources are anticipated, as an add-on percentage, or by number. Allowances should be made for management services companies and the like. Historically, the direct/indirect ratios have been on average, direct 60%, indirect 40%.

Accommodation availability

This has proved to be a critical restraint on offshore installation and hook-up as there is a limited bed availability which adds an additional burden on the planning engineer in getting the crew-mix just right to make the best use of bed space.

Hot working area efficiency loss

Areas considered to be hot working, due to the restrictive use of welding or gas cutting equipment affect normal working efficiency. Working permits need to be obtained. Pipework and vessels often need to be purged to remove flammable or toxic products. Extra care and precautions need to be taken to ensure safety.

Allowances

Allowances may be said to cover events which we know will happen, but cannot be exactly quantified, e.g. errors, damage, design changes.

Contingencies

Contingency differs from allowances in that it covers the totally unknown but has historical significance.

Factorisation – general

The important point with any factorisation/allowance is that each of the elements embodied in the factor is defined, to prevent double allocation and to assist in identifying any element which may have been overlooked.

Planning and cost manager's responsibilities

7.1 Project team manager

Successful planning and cost management, regardless of the organisation or how it is structured, is only as good as the individuals who form the team and their interrelationship with their manager and other external functions.

We can say without fear of contradiction that in general terms a project is not a one-person organisation. It requires a group of individuals working as a team dedicated to achieving specific goals. An important part of that team is its leader and that leader is the manager. A good team can fail to reach its potential if it is poorly led. A good leader on the other hand can turn even a poor team into high achievers. To some extent leadership is an intangible within the individual – his or her charisma – and the rest must be earned. That requires knowledge, skill and proven performance.

The following is a guide to those management areas where that knowledge and skill needs to be demonstrated and put to good effect. For the person new to the post or those who have career development or promotion in mind, these skills are the foundation for achieving that ambition. It is unfortunate that management skills do not come with the title. Not all of the areas defined will involve the cost manager. There are a few exceptions.

7.2 Management interfaces

The following interfaces are areas which are knowledge-oriented but still require skilled handling.

Product interfaces

- Product performance
- Physical location of parts, system of operation, and related systems

Project interfaces

- Contractors
- Management senior and junior

- Information flow upwards and downwards
- Materials management
- Engineering in general terms

Resource interfaces

- Time
- Money
- Manpower
- Facilities
- Equipment
- Material
- Computers and software (information technology)

By developing the ability to manage and control interfaces the manager will be able to:

- Increase equipment utilisation
- Increase performance efficiency
- Reduce project risk elements
- Identify alternatives to problems
- Identify alternatives to conflicts

7.3   Desirable characteristics in a manager

I have often been asked what I look for in a candidate for promotion to a managerial post – a question that can at times be difficult to answer. Almost any bookshop will stock a dozen or more books dealing with the skills required for management, much of which can be boiled down to a few pages, assuming we are able to deduce what the essential ingredients are.

The characteristics which I consider important and would look for in a planning or cost control manager are:

- Flexibility and adaptability
- Significant initiative and leadership
- Aggressiveness, confidence, persuasiveness
- Ambition, activity, forcefulness
- Effective communicator
- Broad scope of personal interests
- Enthusiasm, imagination, spontaneity
- Ability to balance technical solutions with time/cost and human factors
- Organised and disciplined
- Generalist rather than a specialist
- Ability to identify problems

- Willingness to make decisions
- Able to maintain a proper balance in the use of his or her time

Not all managers have the ability to meet all of the criteria mentioned, and those who from this list can identify areas where they fall short have a starting point for improvement.

7.4   Internal and external management selection

When a post becomes vacant, the common debate is whether to make an internal or an external selection. There are of course advantages and disadvantages both ways.

The advantage of an external candidate is the range of other experience that will be brought into the company. This experience should not be underestimated as it prevents 'close breeding of experience' and can add a wider dimension to the company.

The main advantage of advancing an internal candidate is that it provides a performance incentive to other company staff who have the additional benefit of familiarity with company policy and procedures, and who already know the key people. To be selected, their performance would have been proven in live situations.

As mentioned earlier there are advantages both ways, and companies need to fill vacancies from both sectors to gain major benefits.

7.5   Staff relationships

One of the most important characteristics of a good manager is in not only knowing his or her own strengths and weaknesses but also those of his or her staff. In truth, there are few managers who would not say when asked, that they were not totally aware of their staff capabilities. In real terms, experience has shown that there are few who are prepared to take the time, and make the effort, to become fully aware of their staff's potential.

Many managers fall into the category of first world war generals, giving orders, but lacking the essential qualities of leadership. Fortunately that is rapidly changing, due to more informed management training.

Staff need good leadership to perform to their best ability, and this means they need to know what is expected of them in their relationship with their manager. The following are a few points which will help to build a leadership relationship between manager and staff:

- Staff must know what they are supposed to do and what the end product should be
- They must have a clear understanding of what authority they do have and its limitations

- They should know how to relate to other people within and outside their department
- They should know what constitutes a job well done
- They should be informed of their strengths and weaknesses
- They should be informed of corrective action
- They must know you have a genuine interest in them

A good leader will go out of his or her way to give credit for good work where it is due and preferably in front of others outside the department. Where senior management are involved, this not only demonstrates the manager's own confidence but promotes performance within his staff.

7.6   Directing others

Directing others is every manager's function, to implement and see carried out by others, that which is necessary to achieve or exceed set objectives. To do this with any degree of success requires the following steps to be taken.

- Ensuring that the right person is in each post
- Teaching individuals or groups how to fulfil their duties and responsibilities
- Giving others day-to-day instruction and guidance
- Assigning work, responsibility and authority so that others can make maximum use of their abilities
- Giving encouragement
- Holding private discussions with individuals to discuss how they may improve their performance, solve a personal problem, or realise their ambitions
- Seeing that activities are carried out in relation to their importance

Directing therefore involves staffing, training, supervision, delegation, nurturing, counselling and co-ordination. To direct properly, the manager must plan his or her time so that time is made available to meet these obligations.

Some people may be called a manager and are not, and others are not called a manager but they are. **The title of manager deserves the performance of a manager.**

7.7   Planning your time

Planning the best use of your time requires four key elements to be mastered:

- Setting priorities
- Delegation of work

- Organisation
- Personal discipline

It was once thought that if you did not work 60 plus hours a week every week you were not doing your job. Today's thought is that if you have to work 60 plus hours a week, you can't be doing your job.

If the excuse is 'I need to be there to see the job is done properly', then you don't have the right staff or your directing is poor. Should that not be the case and you feel you still must be there, then you do have a problem which you must resolve, and in most cases, it is likely to be caused by inability to manage one's own time and also the inability to delegate the work, for whatever reason.

Improper time management is an activity trap, whereby as a manager, you are controlled by the job rather than you controlling the job. A simple rule is to ask yourself, as an everyday routine, these four questions:

- What am I doing that need not be done at all?
- What am I doing that could be better done by someone else?
- What am I doing that could be done sufficiently well (with a little helpful input) by someone else?
- Have I set the right priorities for my work?

A simple philosophy is to attempt to work yourself out of the job! In this way, you will ensure good delegation, and training of your staff. As time becomes more available, you will have more time to devote to managing your department in a more professional way.

There are, of course, times in the life of any organisation when it is all hands to the pumps, so to speak, and long hours over a short period cannot be avoided. At such times, a well managed team who are well trained in their job can demonstrate their loyalty and ability.

7.8   Driving and restraining forces

The success of any venture, department, or project depends to a great extent on the leader/manager's ability to understand and control a range of opposing forces. By encouraging the positive elements and avoiding the negative forces not only will your performance improve but also that of your staff.

We need to identify what these forces are and how they apply in a working environment, and to do this, the first objective is to separate them out into specific areas and then look at the driving and restraining components which impact on these areas. The most important of these areas are as follows:

- Personal drive
- Team motivation
- Managerial support
- Functional support
- Technical expertise
- Project objectives

Within these areas, we can attempt to define positive and negative elements for each one.

Personal drive

- Driving forces
  - Desire for accomplishment
  - Project interest
  - Work challenge
  - Group acceptance
  - Common objectives
- Restraining forces
  - Poor leadership
  - Uncertain roles
  - Lack of technical knowledge
  - Personality problems

Team motivation

- Driving forces
  - Good interpersonal relationships
  - Desire to achieve
  - Expertise
  - Common goal
- Restraining forces
  - Poor organisation
  - Communication barriers
  - Poor leadership
  - Uncertain rewards
  - Uncertain objectives

Managerial support

- Driving forces
  - Sufficient resources

- – Proper priorities
- – Authority delegation
- – Management interest
- Restraining forces
  - – Unclear objectives
  - – Insufficient resources
  - – Changing priorities
  - – Lack of authority
  - – Lack of support
  - – Management indifference

Functional support

- Driving forces
  - – Clear goals and priorities
  - – Good planning and cost control techniques
  - – Good technical guidance and support
  - – Adequate task supervision
  - – Proper staff training
- Restraining forces
  - – Priority conflicts
  - – Funding restraints
  - – Lack of technical guidance
  - – Poor project organisation
  - – Lack of interest

Technical expertise

- Driving forces
  - – Ability to manage the technology
  - – Prior track record
  - – Low risk project
  - – Good technical information flow
- Restraining forces
  - – Lack of technical information
  - – Unexpected technical problems
  - – Inability to cope with change

Project objectives

- Driving forces
  - – Clear goals
  - – Clear expectations/responsibilities

- – Clear interface relationships
- – Clear specifications
- Restraining forces
  - – Conflict over objectives
  - – Company uncertainties
  - – Prolonged decision-making

With a clear understanding of these driving and restraining forces, and acting on them, the manager will be able to establish the first and most important interrelationship – that with his or her staff.

7.9   Organisational power play

At the start of any project there is a shuffling for position by many of the senior staff, attempting to find favour with the project manager, senior executive or whatever. This behaviour should be viewed with amusement and participation should be avoided at all costs. As the planning or cost control manager the project manager relies on your output for presentation to the board. As such your importance within the organisation is guaranteed, and there is no need to get involved in power struggles.

It is unfortunate but true, if the project manager does not have a good relationship with planning and cost personnel, his post cannot be sustained for any length of time. To become involved in power politics will only generate conflicts. As a manager who is dealing with all disciplines in every phase of the project, it is necessary to maintain good working relationships with all project staff and therefore unnecessary conflicts should be avoided. Always try to be part of the solution and not the problem.

It is worth remembering that promotions based on politics/favouritism are perilous and are seldom long lasting. Promotion based on performance can at times be a bit slower but is much more enduring.

7.10   Corporate planning and cost procedures

When developing specific project procedures, the manager should take as his guide those procedures already issued by the corporate functions. The corporate procedures will have the approval of the management and should be based on tried and tested methods. In general terms, they should need only minor modification to tailor them to meet the specific project needs. Should a major change be required to some areas of the procedure, functional approval should be obtained. To do otherwise is to court disfavour or worse.

7.11   Functional support

Problems arise on all projects, be they technical, managerial, or resource related, where there is a need to seek assistance or advice. It is the role of the corporate function manager to help and give support in such cases and he or she is a resource worth using. Do not allow yourself to become isolated within a project because introverted management only leads to major problems now or in the future.

7.12   Hiring of staff

The method of hiring staff varies from company to company depending on the specific employment procedure. The question facing the manager is whether the person being hired should form part of the company's permanent staff or be drawn from the agency pool. Once the approval to fill a vacancy has been granted, the manager has a staff obligation depending on the category of the person filling the vacant post.

As a general rule no permanent staff should be hired by the project without the approval of the company, as the company has a long-term obligation to its permanent employees. Projects are of a limited duration and on completion of the project, the company would be responsible for the engineer's gainful employment, training, promotional aspects and so on.

The screening and proposal of a candidate is normally standard practice as is the attendance of any candidate for interview for any post, be it of a permanent or temporary nature. In the case of temporary contract staff the company's obligation is limited, and should the person/s not perform to the project requirements, they can be easily released.

7.13   Assistant manager

The post of assistant may or may not exist within your organisation, but it is still important to select a deputy who can function as the manager in your absence. Selection of a deputy should be made with some care and attention, ensuring they have the skills to carry out the various functions. A manager should attempt to strengthen any areas of weakness by giving advice and instruction. Once selected, the individual should be aware of all your actions which relate to the project directly and indirectly.

7.14   External relationships

In parallel to the development of departmental good relations, the manager must maintain good relationships with external disciplines and function. These external bodies are a major source of information which is necessary to carry out successfully the everyday tasks. There is also a need to support these bodies with information to allow them to perform their tasks with a degree of efficiency. To maintain an appropriate cross-flow of information, the manager needs to be aware of how these departments interrelate, a subject we will be dealing with next.

8

Project planning and cost engineering relationships

8.1 Fundamental relationship

There is no doubt that to develop and maintain the optimum balance between time, cost and resources to meet project objectives, an integrated planning/cost engineering approach is necessary. This is a simple enough aim and in truth is not difficult to do if planning and cost engineers, aided by accountants, work together.

8.2 Money – an activity resource

If we consider cost, that is the funds estimated to do the work, as a resource, we can then relate it to the specific network activity to which it applies. Once we have achieved this objective we have the ability to place these costs in time, which is a fundamental requirement of any planning and cost integration programme. Almost all of today's project management software has been developed to make this task an easy one and also able to maintain the budget security aspects. Relating costs is no different from the way we allocate a trade group to an activity, see Fig. 8.1.

To ensure this integration is successful we need to adopt a systematic and understanding approach. This will be discussed in more detail later but for the moment we require an overview of the basics.

8.3 Global estimate

The global estimate establishes a 'first cut' figure for time, duration, resources, and cost setting the initial parameters. The generation of the parameters should be established using a simplified work breakdown (summary level network activities) and applying global norms for both planning and cost such as man-hours/tonne, and major equipment costs, the norms being taken from past company history of similar work. These estimates can again be compared with historical data to ensure the initial results are within acceptable limits.

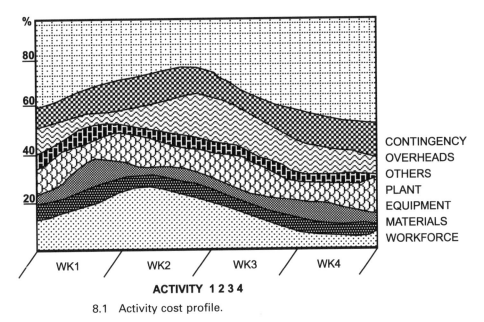

8.1   Activity cost profile.

The global estimates should highlight areas which may be in error and allow modification, if necessary, before final commitment in principle.

8.4   High level estimate breakdown

On management acceptance of the global estimate in principle the major activities can then be broken down into a more defined work breakdown structure. On completion of this more definitive breakdown of activities, and associated costs, a code of accounts can be allocated. Using this as a base a more exact estimate can be prepared by cost and planning groups, as information becomes available. The code of accounts can be generated automatically by some software packages and allow the formation of a code of accounts 'Dictionary'.

8.5   Logic networks and cost allocation

In parallel to estimating breakdown of activities and forming the basis of the cost structure planning should prepare a summary level network to establish the initial time, resource and cost allocation parameters. The summary network must be examined by cost engineering to make sure that there are sufficient activities addressed to give a reasonable high level cost structure. Agreement between planning and cost engineering at this stage is fundamental.

8.6   Schedules and initial goals

Having completed the logic networks, and applied man-hour and duration information, the network can be processed to obtain an optimum schedule or schedules. The schedules at this point would form a common working tool. The schedule will highlight all the company goals and form a major information source and discussion document. In the early stages of project development or project tendering a 'broad brush' approach can assist management in their decision-making and general project familiarisation.

8.7   Estimate phasing/budgets/AFEs

Using the schedules developed, cost engineering will now be able to phase costs across the project duration and produce budgets and AFEs (see p. 100) in line with the work breakdown structure/code of accounts.

In practice, cost engineering would maintain on their own computer system a copy of the high level networks, containing additional cost data so as to maintain confidentiality. It is also common practice for cost engineering to add additional activities for the purpose of phasing such items as overheads and other expenditures which are not necessary for 'job' planning. Again a number of the cost management software packages which integrate with the scheduling software, make provision for 'cost spreading'.

8.8   Progress measurement – the critical function

Progress measurement is probably the most important function in project control. Progress attained is the catalyst for schedule and resource analysis, cost analysis, accounts, material delivery and logistics. As such it takes a high priority with regard to control management.

It is generally part of the planning function to be responsible for the measurement of actual physical progress. The **actual** progress would then be compared against that which was originally planned. The results of the comparison analysis, coupled with the man-hour expenditure would then be collated in a manner suited to the planning and cost systems.

8.9   Expenditure statements related to actuals

Using the man-hour expenditure, materials and overhead costs, cost engineering would be able to produce statements of expenditure to date. This analysis would be presented in graphical and tabular form, comparing present cost against budget and indicating future trends.

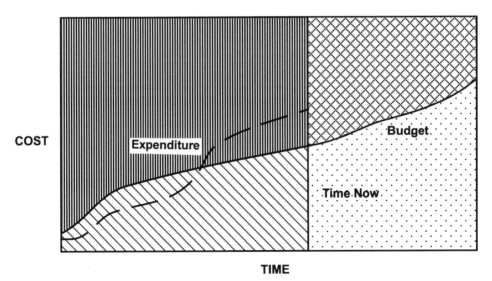

8.2   Simplified cost analysis.

What we must avoid is misrepresentation, even with simple graphical presentations, ensuring that what we present gives a **true picture**.

If, as shown in Fig. 8.2, the present forecast/budget was an earlier generation than the actual, the overspend may be caused as a result of being ahead on progress. In this case we could find that we do not have a problem. On the other hand, if we were behind on progress the overspend could be much more than indicated. We are only able to see the true picture when both elements are of the same generation. This highlights the fact that no cost analysis is of real value unless it is linked directly to planning/progress measurement.

Reading a cost report can have its own problems if you are unaware of even some of the simpler terms, and what they mean. In some cases there are slight differences in interpretation from one project to another. To clear this point up the following is a general explanation to the more commonly used definitions.

Latest approved budget

The latest budget that has been considered and approved by the authorising body.

Budget

The budget is the total funds allocated for the implementation and completion of the project or for specific elements of the project.

It takes into account the defined scope of work and associate schedule. It will also include all forms of appropriate allowances and contingencies.

Incurred cost

The value of work done to date, or within a specific period. It will include cash paid, invoices received but unpaid, and accrual of costs incurred but not invoiced.

Estimate to completion

The estimated funds to complete the project over and above the incurred costs. It is based on a general assessment of all the information related to the outstanding scope of work. The assessment should include but not be limited to, commitment to date, trends in project progress and performance, trends in scope changes, trends in escalation, contract claims and so on.

Anticipated final cost

The sum of the incurred costs to date and the estimate to completion.

Variance

The difference between the approved budget and the anticipated final cost.

Authorisation for expenditure (AFE)

The AFE is a procedural document which records the approval of management for the release of funds to the project manager. The funds are released for the implementation of a specific project proposal that is within the constraints of the defined scope and approved budget.

Commitment

Commitment is achieved when an agreement is concluded between buyer and supplier. The extent of that commitment and value is defined by the commercial arrangements included in the documentation. Commitment includes items such as purchase orders, letters of intent, service agreements and contract documents.

Base estimate

The estimate of the cost of a defined scope of work which was valid at the time of estimation excluding escalation, and may or may not include contingency.

Contingency

A specific monetary allowance within an estimate for unforeseeable occurrences, which statistics indicate is likely to be required. It allows for such items as estimating error, omissions or poorly defined scope and schedule slippage.

Escalation

An evaluation of the future effects of inflation on the base cost of the prepared budget.

Current budget

The latest approved budget plus the cost of any additions, modifications, or deletions due to scope changes, approved by the project manager but not as yet by the management or committee, as the case may be.

Planned value of work (schedule)

The distribution of the budget linked to the network activities accurately phased in accordance with planned project progress and consumption of resources.

Planned value of work accomplished

The budget value of the work achieved to date in accordance with progress measurement.

8.10   Time and man-hour forecasts

From the progress figures and man-hour expenditure a comparison can be made between planned and actual progress. This comparison will result in **project performance factors** being established. By using these factors and applying them to the work still to be done we can establish the latest time and man-hour forecasts.

In some cases if an overrun is predicted, we will be able to increase the resources to maintain the time period, in others with restricted access the time period may have to be extended and rescheduling of time elements will be necessary. Extended time periods may mean we will be able to divert resources from less critical resources and so on. Computer software comes into its own here, having the ability to run a multitude of scenarios in a few minutes to find the optimum answer.

These factors are often referred to as productivity **which they are not!** Let us assume for a moment that a job has been underestimated at ten man-hours when it should have been allocated twenty. If the work is completed in twenty hours the resultant productivity would be 50% or 0.5 depending on how you want to present it, but the true productivity is 100%. The reverse could also be the case if the job was overestimated. What we are really calculating is the **estimating accuracy** using this particular workforce on this project in this location at this time of year.

It is also for the possibility of estimating inaccuracies that performance calculations need to cover a range of activities. The greater the population the more representative the figures will be or 'swings and roundabouts' as some would say. The factors should wherever possible be applied on a discipline basis. Experience has shown that one trade estimating group may have made a very good estimate and others working with another discipline a poor estimate.

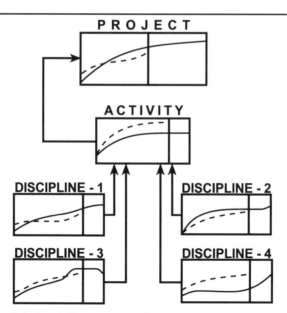

8.3 Discipline aggregration.

8.11 Costs forecasts related to performance

The planning forecasts using the latest performance factors can be calculated and costs applied to produce forecast costs to complete and anticipated expenditure profiles.

Ideally, for ease of understanding, these profiles should be presented in an accumulative graphical structure with tabular back-up. Presenting this type of information by major activity and discipline for ongoing work has a number of analytical advantages. In this way any negative variations can be traced to the specific trade group, i.e. Discipline – 4, as shown in the simplified example of Fig. 8.3, and remedial action taken.

In the case of progress measurement, the same principle would apply where a discipline analysis is required. If, for example, the activity level graph indicated a saving, we may be convinced to look no further, and may miss a decline in a specific discipline because the efficiency of the other activity disciplines acts to support the decline. The variations both positive and negative can be extensive, and need to be viewed to ensure that should remedial action be required, the effort is properly directed.

Importance of materials management

9.1 Materials management – a major task

An example of the importance of materials management is clearly demonstrated when we look at the cost of equipment and materials related to any major onshore or offshore project. Historically, the value of these purchases is on average 15–25% of the total project cost, with deliveries spread over the entire project duration.

The scope and variety of materials management work on projects of this type is immense and can include the placing of over 1000 major purchases. Orders may cover the supply of some 30000 tonnes of steel, 100 km of assorted piping, 1200 km of cabling and 75000 items of pipe fittings. In addition to these bulk materials there is the process plant, generation equipment, civil materials, lifting and materials handling equipment and so on. **Good materials management is one of the cornerstones within any project.**

9.2 Integrating materials management information

Materials management within a project generates a considerable amount of information vital to project cost and planning. This information relating to the acquisition, allocation and distribution of project materials/equipment, plays a major role in the process of managerial decision-making. Without the timely supply and control of the right materials it would be impossible to achieve project objectives successfully. Materials management is, therefore, a key function in the favourable execution of any project.

9.3 Need for co-ordination

The substantial influence exercised by materials management on the project cost and time schedules is clearly indicated. What this reveals is that a strong interrelationship should be established and maintained between cost, planning and materials management, with respect to material/equipment costs and delivery requirements. Maintenance of an up-to-date, accurate expenditure and delivery programme, depends on the good cross-flow of information between the functions. The information related to materials increases steadily, as a project progresses through its various phases from a forecast of possible delivery dates and costs for long-lead items at the start of a project, through to a much more detailed delivery schedule and related costs during the detailed design and construction phases.

9.4   Defining materials management

Various incorrect terms are often used to identify the materials management function. The most common of these misnomers is 'purchasing' or 'procurement' which are functions within materials management. **Materials management may be defined as** *the confederacy of traditional materials activities bound by a common integrated approach to the cost, planning, acquisition, flow and distribution of project materials.*

Materials management function responsibilities may be considered to include:

- Purchasing
- Traffic
- Inspection
- Materials control
- Expediting

9.5   Interaction of materials management

Cost/planning/materials management interaction occurs throughout the life of a project, which covers three general phases each with their own specific requirements.

- Pre-project phase
- Engineering phase
- Construction phase

The following guideline broadly outlines salient areas of interrelated activities, covering all project phases, and indicates cost and planning requirements from the materials management system.

9.6   Co-ordination requirements (materials)

Materials management of capital projects follows two basic routes:

- A substantial amount of project materials management is carried out by the company in cases where there is free issue of equipment and constructional materials to contractors

- Main subcontractors perform the foregoing task as part of an overall brief

In both cases the co-ordination requirements between cost/planning and materials management are basically the same, the information required coming from different sources.

9.7   Pre-project phase (materials)

For a project to be considered viable, ideas must become more perceptible. Part of this perceptibility, and to assist in project feasibility, is the development of the preliminary cost and schedule report.

A major part of both these reports relies on obtaining possible materials delivery dates and up-to-date costs. This information is essential for the scheduling of activities and preliminary material costs for budgeting. To be able to satisfy the cost and schedule needs, a minimum level of information is required.

- Forecast of anticipated cost
- Forecast of deliveries for major or critical equipment/materials
- Forecast of standard materials management cycle activities i.e. procurement, inspection and shipment

The information required from materials management is, therefore, of a global nature, derived from current information and/or historical data.

The programmes and cost information produced during this phase are used for the generation of early budgets and probable durations of major activities, milestones, target production dates and so on. The exchange of information during this phase is minimal and mainly restricted to global procurement data. Most of the interaction is conducted at a personal level, and therefore a formalised format of co-ordination is not generally required.

9.8   Engineering phase (materials)

The cost and planning function becomes more active once a project is given the 'go-ahead'. The pace of informational exchange starts to build up and the accuracy requirement on information increases. Frequency of interaction between the functions also increases considerably, due to the evolutionary and recursive nature of cost and planning.

The engineering phase is considered to include all project design engineering activities starting from front-end through to the end of detailed design. With the development of design, and the acquisition of hard data, detailed cost analysis and programmes with higher confidence factors can be produced. Greater demands are now made on the materials management section covering not only a more accurate cost and delivery forecast but details of how the various tasks will be managed. The type of information required to develop detailed budgets and schedules will be as follows:

- Materials management operational philosophy
- Materials distribution plan
- Project standard materials management cycles/logic
- Equipment and materials delivery estimates
- Potential problems likely to delay deliveries
- Shipping and traffic requirements/durations
- Project standard purchasing requirements (i.e. vendor assessment, bid invitation, bid evaluation, purchase order award, and costs)
- Project standard inspection requirements
- Progress feedback from vendors and control of approved project programmes
- Vendor information for feedback into design programmes

9.9   Construction phase (materials)

The construction phase occupies a relatively larger portion of the project time frame and consequently has a marked influence on the overall duration and successful execution of a project. The construction phase would normally include the following project activities:

- On-site construction
- Fabrication and pre-commissioning
- Installation and systems hook-up
- Commissioning/mechanical completion

Materials management activities during the construction phase are mainly related to expenditure, traffic and physical control of materials/equipment at various sites. The purchasing activity will have diminished but the expediting and quality assurance aspects of the outstanding materials will now become critical functions.

Construction performance will be affected by late delivery of equipment, and also to a large extent by the restricted flow of bulk materials should it occur. It is therefore essential that close co-ordination should be maintained to ensure availability of the proper materials in the required quantities, at the right time. Materials management therefore needs to know what is the right time, ROS dates well in advance, and not only the right time but the budget allocated price if they are to set internal control parameters. The source of this information is the cost and planning documentation.

9.10   Cost and planning related to materials

Most of the cost and planning documents are developed and established well before the start of the construction phase. Updates on project equipment/materials deliveries are made available to materials management on a daily/weekly and monthly basis. Cost and planning functional activities are largely related to monitoring and control, requiring continuous materials, expediting, delivery and inventory information for updating purposes.

A typical range of information required from materials management during the construction phase would be:

* Materials stock status
* Purchase order status
* Expediting status
* Materials/equipment QA status
* In transit status
* Site material status
* Vendor bids status
* Price changes status

9.11   General requirements for co-ordination

We can see from the foregoing that materials, planning, and cost need to maintain a close relationship and also that some guidelines, as to how this is achieved, are required. The way this is achieved is through a co-ordination procedure, which is necessary if cost and planning are to produce a budget and a programme which conforms to the concept and philosophy of a project in general. If they are to be of any value, co-ordination procedures must be based on compatible thinking. If they are not, they will be discarded or circumvented and this applies to all procedures.

Compatibility of information exchange and co-ordination effort is very important. Information received from various sources on the project is used by cost and planning to carry out their functional responsibilities. It is therefore vital that information received from materials management is compatible with requirements and presented in a format for ease of assimilation.

As a guide, here are some of the salient points worth considering when producing detailed co-ordination procedures (the points should be agreed between two functions during project start-up):

* Type of information required
* Frequency of information exchange
* Method of information exchange
* Organisation of information exchange
* Material management stages

- Representation of materials management activities on project networks
- Materials/equipment distribution

The accuracy of information required varies considerably from phase to phase. Generally the demand on accuracy increases as a project gains momentum and passes from development to engineering and construction phases. The driving force behind this requirement is the need to produce more definite cost analysis, programmes and schedules.

9.12   Materials control as it relates to planning and cost control

As mentioned earlier, planning and cost functions rely heavily on materials management for delivery and cost information. To meet these demands, materials management needs to ensure the development, implementation and maintenance of adequate materials control procedures and systems. These procedures exist to provide the much needed information with the minimum of turn-round time. Due to the bulk of materials involved the control mechanism needs to be geared to cater for the volume, delivery and geographical spread of procurement activities, stores and sites.

9.13   Vendor control system (planning related)

The majority of items required by a project are obtained from a myriad of vendors and this requires an efficient control mechanism. Materials management, in collaboration with planning, should ensure that vendors' planning and progressing procedures are adequate and compatible with project planning requirements. To ensure that the vendors are aware of their obligation, suitable clauses should be incorporated in purchase orders to confirm the availability of the required information.

Materials management generates and deals with a large quantity of project documents which have a direct bearing on cost and planning activities. Many of the documents will be required long after the project is complete to provide, if required, 'audit' trails for materials and equipment supplied. Managing these documents is not a simple task and therefore materials management systems should include procedures providing control over purchasing, inspection, certification, traffic and stores documentation.

Required-on-site (ROS) dates

For obvious reasons, one of the first things the purchasing department needs to know is when the item will be required on-site. ROS dates directly control the project from the design phase through to construction completion. Once established they control to a major extent the sequence of the work. It is therefore a very critical function within the planning section to establish the ROS dates. ROS dates are derived from the construction schedule early start dates. Procurement can then establish by subtraction of fabrication and delivery times the PO (purchase order) date which in turn sets the timescale for design completion of each item. It is therefore incumbent upon project planning to inform cost engineering and materials management of the ROS dates for major materials and equipment as early as possible. Never set ROS dates by working from the design phase forward as this leads to a project with no clear sequence of activities.

Advance delivery period

In the early part of the design phase it is common practice to set the ROS dates for long-lead items two months in advance of the envisaged site requirement, and as these requirements become progressively firmer, the ROS dates aligned to one month in advance of the subcontractor's schedule need date (SND).

Setting the advance delivery period

In setting the advance delivery period there are a few precautions we should consider. **Too long** an advance delivery period gives rise to:

- Weather damage, pilfering and loss
- Damage due to excessive handling (plate materials)
- Degrading of markings

If in doubt, remember it is **better to be looking at it than for it**. **Too short** an advance period gives rise to:

- An inferior product through undue pressure on the supplier
- A limit on forward production and construction planning due to a lack of material visibility
- Insufficient time for final quality control examination of the product and consequently, delayed paperwork

All of the above have a cost implication.

10.1 Procedures and objectives

The importance of developing company documentation in the form of a procedure is to provide a series of approved guidelines. From these guidelines can be derived detailed project procedures, thereby ensuring a consistent approach. Before a guideline/procedure is produced, the scope and influence of the document need to be thoroughly understood.

Before preparing any procedure, and also before we can hope to manage a department effectively, time should be taken to define the objectives we want to achieve. These objectives should relate to all personnel, from site engineer through to the departmental manager. Each person, in their own way and within their sphere of influence, has the responsibility to plan the work by setting related objectives. An example of these objectives which may be used within the planning section would be as follows:

1) To prepare a plan which gives an accurate assessment of the logic, time and resources necessary to meet the project's technical requirements, calendar, cost and safety parameters.
2) To closely monitor all aspects of a project, inform management of its status and establish progress trends to enable preventive or corrective action to be taken if required.
3) To validate contractor, subcontractor or vendors' planning and schedules, and to ensure the proper application of agreed co-ordination procedures.
4) To present clear and concise planning documentation in a readily understood format to various levels of management.

These four objectives cover the principal roles of the planning engineer. It would be possible to add a few more but it is my own view that they would be more cosmetic than practical.

Part of the setting of objectives and the subsequent development of procedure is having an understanding of the importance of relative information. The quality of any plan depends on two things, the skill of the planning engineer and the information he or she has to work with. Major projects are not only complicated but also technically demanding. To ensure the best possible plan which has a high probability of success relies on all functions and disciplines lending their co-operation and experience in the formation of the plan.

No one engineer, or for that matter group of engineers, will be apprised of all aspects of a project, and left to their own devices, may create a planning error – an error which could turn out to be very costly.

How often do we hear a department or section complain about the plan/schedule when the project is underway but were reluctant to co-operate at the plan's inception?

It is worth noticing that management at times is often resistant to the employment of additional personnel for departments which they feel are sufficiently staffed – a judgement which is very hard to make unless you are directly involved in the work. When staff become overstretched, errors can and do occur in situations which, in monetary terms, would probably support additional staff salaries ten times over.

10.2   Information and assumptions (planning)

In the preparation of a plan, the planning engineer requires specific levels of information to provide meaningful results. The absence of information means that the planning engineer will be required to make assumptions based on his own experience, historical data and the section's experience. No matter how good these assumptions are, the fact that assumptions exist within a plan increases the risk factor, due to possible inaccuracies.

All assumptions are not critical. Even what may be termed a major error may only result in a few additional man-hours but there are other errors which can have dramatic impact on the scheduling, on resources and on cost. It is the assumptions with potentially serious impact that we must be aware of and carefully monitor, seeking factual information so as to remove them from the assumption category.

The only time we can hope to know all the facts is at project completion. When we plan a project from day one, we are aware that it is a best guess, and hope that it is a good one. The weather being worse than average, more deliveries than anticipated being late, a need for a change in design at a critical phase causing a setback, plant breakdown, labour problems and a host of other incidentals can defeat even the best-laid plan. Add a lack of good information to these possible stumbling blocks, and it is only luck if a project remains within schedule and cost. However, with good information and a few good assumptions, a project has a fighting chance of reaching its goals.

The key fact is that, the more information available, the more accurate will be the planning schedule/forecast. The early phases of any project will contain inaccuracies due to the varying levels of fixed and hard data available, which will result in corresponding degrees of schedule, resource, and cost risks.

To create a workable and reliable programme it is necessary to define the risk associated with the level of information available and at a particular stage of overall project development. Activities which are at risk should be noted and the assumptions made listed for future reference in the form of work sheets.

The time is long gone, or do I mean should be gone, when planning calculations were done 'on the back of an envelope', so to speak. Like any other major document, it must be possible to audit the source of the calculations should negative variation of any significance occur. The best way to achieve this is to generate a work sheet/information listing, either computer-generated or handwritten. Information listing need only apply to the high level planning. Detail planning generates its own 'listings' in the form of job cards, work sheets, system tracking and monitoring.

It is the responsibility of the planning engineer to develop, as early as possible, his or her own listing for each activity, its duration and how resources were derived. This may be in the form of a high level WBS (work breakdown structure). Where assumptions or best guesses have been made, they should be noted, as they will need to be clarified some time in the future as information becomes available.

Where activities require external input, the engineer should ensure that those responsible for supplying the information are informed at the earliest possible moment, so that they can provide an answer in good time.

A danger does occur with software which is easily manipulated, and where no record is kept of changes, or where changes go unaudited, or unchallenged. It is a simple matter, for the inexperienced, to 'plan' a financial disaster unknowingly, in an attempt to improve the schedule.

The simplest form of this type of schedule 'improvement' would be to extend a non-critical duration, in an attempt to maintain, or level a resource, and to forget they have extended the hire of a major piece of plant. This is not so uncommon a fault as you may think, and it may not even be immediately obvious if the plant, for example, is a wall of scaffolding, a crane or cranes, or earth-moving equipment. The cost of a few more workforce wages may be well outweighed by the cost of the plant hire.

11.1 Control plan concept

The project control plan is a management-endorsed series of documents defining in broad terms the company's approach to the control of the project, the general philosophy, system, execution plan and programming style. Within the control plan, the schedule and financial objectives of the project must reflect both previous experience and current conditions if they are to provide meaningful and achievable goals. It is in this context that the project control plan approach has proved so effective in the execution of high-technology, high-cost projects.

The fundamental objective of project control is to provide management with the means to achieve project execution within fixed time and cost restraints. The major parameters defining a project are scope, cost, time, resources, materials, as shown in Fig. 11.1, and productivity. Project control will achieve its objective by linking these six parameters to a single common factor, the network activity.

By definition, a network activity is an element in the series of logically-linked tasks required to achieve project goals. An activity will be the lowest level of work element within a project. The scope, cost, time, resources and materials required for the actual performance of each network activity are used as the basis for an effective, integrated project control system.

The art of project control is in the ability to efficiently and accurately analyse measured progress, and compare the results against plans/schedules. Where negative variation exists, take preventive or corrective action, as necessary. To be able to conduct efficient progress monitoring, measuring and reporting a system of operation which will meet the necessary criteria is therefore essential. The system, to be effective and to be universally understood by those who must administer and work within it, must be fully described. What follows is an attempt to describe a typical system and its application view from the planning standpoint starting with the project execution plan.

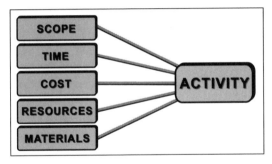

11.1   Activity components.

11.2   Project execution plan

Planning's prime function is to provide a service to the project and company management by supplying them with project tasks, programmes and performance information. The basis of the execution plan is the information which will be provided, how it will be derived and its function. When writing an instruction of this sort, we need to avoid words like could, would, may, and use words like will and must. To allow any unnecessary loopholes in the instruction is to court non-compliance.

For the benefit of the reader, the sample instruction given will be presented in a manner similar to that which may be expected in a company document. A typical execution plan would be similar to the following.

11.3   Project programmes

All project programmes will be developed using deterministic critical path network techniques. In addition, probabilistic analysis techniques such as Monte Carlo statistical simulation risk management will be used, as and when required. Project networks will be analysed using an approved computer software package, suitable for linking to the integrated project management system.

In this case we are making sure that there is a project logic which can be presented as a precedence or arrow network from which we can check the logical sequencing of the work.

11.4   Programme tiers

A tiered structure of network programmes will be developed, to ensure integration between work areas and project phases, and to provide sufficient information at various levels of project and company management. *Generally, a three-tiered network suite will be required for a project.*

The three levels of network programmes will be:

- Level I   Master network
- Level II   Project control network
- Level III Working networks

The network is of more use to the planning engineer for logic checks than senior management. Senior management, in my experience, can make better use of a logic linked bar chart mirroring the programme levels.

11.5   Schedule classification and phasing

When reviewing a network, schedule or the like, it is important to know just what the classification is, as this relates directly to the risk. The risk not only has a bearing on the completion date but also in the maintaining of the budget. As part of the execution plan a classification system should be devised.

To facilitate schedule reviewing, and fixing the elements of risk in meeting schedule criteria, within limits, schedules are classified into the following groups:

E – Pre-project phase
D – Project start-up phase
C – Preliminary project phase
B – Detail design phase
A – Construction phase

From the company's experience in project schedule and cost accuracy, it should be possible to allocate a percentage which could be set against each of the classified groups.

To assist in measuring and reporting, and for the development of historical data statistics, a project can be divided into a series of phases, as follows:

- Development (from concept until the start of design)
- Engineering (all work related to the design aspects)
- Construction (construction of components including civil works)
- Installation (installation of all equipment and systems)
- Commissioning (testing all systems and components; preparing mechanical completion documentation ready for handover)

Most projects, no matter how large, can be covered by these five major phases. With projects which are not of a construction type, a group of phases should be devised to suit the project. To facilitate progress measurement and reporting, project phases will be clearly defined with a finite start and finish. A suite of networks will be developed and maintained to cover each project phase in which the company is involved.

11.6   Work element breakdown structure

Not so many years ago, the work breakdown structure used extensively today, was a new concept. That original concept has matured to what it is today. Activities at a high level are too large, and too complex, to be tackled in one large unit. To complete an activity, in a logical and practical way, it must be broken down into manageable components/work elements. The work elements in turn can be further broken down into trade tasks in the form of job cards, task or job sheets or equivalent.

Sub-division of work is essential to bring major activities down to work-able size units for the trades to cope with. Excessive sub-division on the other hand can result in confusion and a loss of control. Computers can handle very large volumes of detail but can we understand it, remember it, or act on it?

11.7   Progress measurement and reporting

Progress of every identifiable project activity will be measured in order to report and assess the viability of achieving target completion dates, throughout the project life. The productivity of each function's work area will be calculated to provide a realistic base for trend analysis, and to assess the validity of the forecasts. *The need for accurate progress reporting cannot be over-emphasised, as it is the keystone supporting all the project functions. It is therefore necessary to be explicit, when addressing progress reporting, within the project control plan.*

Progress reporting parameters will be carefully selected for ease of planning, scheduling and progress measurement. Procedures have been developed to ensure that the selected parameters are properly estimated, programmed, monitored, measured, and reported. A variety of progress reports will be produced at various levels of detail, to provide suitable and sufficient information required by the different levels of management, to advise them of the project position, and to assist where necessary in decision-making. Progress reporting will cover all areas, functions, and phases of a project.

A typical progress report, produced by project planning, should comprise the following four sections:

- Summary/synopsis
- Narrative
- Statistical/graphical
- Recommendation

As a rule, reports should be brief, concise and based on exceptions.

11.8 Organisation

It is important within the control plan to be positive about the allocation of staff, as this is a working document for the planning manager, and an authority to place staff. Project planning representatives will be assigned to key areas associated with the development of the project, and will control individual planning operations. Their duties will include reporting on progress, materials, resources and areas of variance and suggesting remedial action.

Planning engineers, together with cost control, material control and estimating engineers, will be assigned to a project and will be responsible to the project manager through the line management (normally the project planning and cost manager or managers) for their day-to-day activities.

Overall project planning, incorporating all phases of a project, will be directed by the project manager. *Here we specify the relationship the engineer has to the project manager so that there will be no confusion. The company or corporate planning manager will ensure that the work is carried out in a professional way and within the company guidelines, also rendering assistance and guidance.*

Having laid out the basic requirements, within the project control plan, it is now possible to define these areas further, under the headings of:

- Project programming
- Schedule support information
- Work scope definition
- Progress monitoring

As we move through the following chapters we will be able to build on these headings defining in detail the specific functional requirements to meet the project need.

12

Cost estimating and control

12.1 General principles

For any project to be successful, it must meet both the client and company cost parameters. The client's goal is to complete a project in time within his or her allowed/allocated budget. The company's aim is to obtain a reasonable price for the work which will also result in a fair profit. This allows the company to stay in business, and remain as a viable resource to the client and industry in general.

To meet these requirements is a two-phased function:

- Establishing a realistic cost estimate
- Controlling the cost once established

The goals are clear enough and uncomplicated. Unfortunately obtaining them is not! It takes knowledge, skill, understanding, and more than a modicum of experience. The title 'cost engineer' as opposed to 'cost accountant' tells its own story. The cost engineer to be able to competently estimate, allocate and control costs, must have an in-depth knowledge of the technical aspects of the project and must maintain a wide range of interrelationships to meet the requirements of cost estimating and budget preparation. These relationships need to be maintained throughout the life of the project to enable monitoring and control of project costs.

In principle cost estimating is simple; list the elements required to complete the project and put a price to them, the sum of the cost being the cost estimate. Unfortunately, this is not like going down to your local supermarket with a defined list of purchases and finding all the items already priced and on the shelves. It is more like going down to the supermarket with a bit of a list and having to guess the price of many of the items but still bring back all you will need and for the money you have been given.

The difficulty arises in the need to **list the elements** because some elements can be seen in the form of materials, plant, manpower resources etc and some, like taxes, cannot be seen. In order to formulate a comprehensive list of elements, it is necessary to approach the task in an orderly and logical way and to seek guidance. This is normally achieved by the use of the company cost procedure which establishes not only the method and systematic approach to be adopted but details many, if not all, of the unseen elements. When we allocate a cost to all the elements, we have the bones of the project budget. It can be termed the bones simply because the company management will need to be consulted as to their specialised input.

12.2 Project budget

The project budget is one of the major yardsticks from which we can control and monitor the efficiency and viability of the project, which with the best will in the world is not an easy task. If it were, history would not have recorded so many dramatic overruns. It would be a simplistic get-out to make the cost engineer a scapegoat and to say in such overrun situations 'the work was underestimated'. It is not, of course, always the fault of the cost engineer, if this happens. There may have been a lack of scope definition, there may have been a managerial price control to obtain the work, there may have been a lack of performance within the workforce. It would certainly have been poor management, and it may be a combination of all these negative elements.

We should not appear too negative at this point, as the bulk of projects which remain within the budget or run over budget by a few per cent far outweighs the major overruns.

The project budget is derived from two basic but complex components:

* Base estimate
* Contingency

Base estimate

All estimates as the word suggests, are a 'best guess' but the important thing to remember is it should be the **best** guess. In the preparation of the estimate of the base cost, all known elements need to be catered for, and wherever possible, the most recent prices obtained for 'hard items', i.e. materials and equipment. A bill of quantities covering the known and anticipated scope should be prepared in consultation with but not limited to the following sectors:

* Engineering
* Construction
* Planning
* Procurement

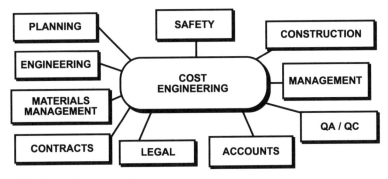

12.1   Cost department interfaces.

- Contracts
- QA/QC
- Legal
- Safety

From the information gathered from these various sources, as shown in Fig. 12.1, the scope can be established and the cost associated with each item, activity, function and resource can be calculated.

As a guide to the components associated with the calculations, the calculations should cover the following categories which may be appropriate in the development of the costs:

- Purchase price
- Transport
- Storage and handling
- Associated man-hours
- Currency exchange
- Insurance
- Tax
- Special services
- Inspection
- Travel
- Documentation
- Fabrication
- Installation
- Test and commissioning
- Surface protection
- Rentals
- Marine related costs (if appropriate)
- Management
- Others

- Contingency allocation (required for the project budget)
- Commercial

The results of the associated cost allocations will form the budget. In practice, one of the best ways to present the budget information is as a spreadsheet, which accommodates easy checking and review. The back-up documentation showing the method of calculation, information source and so on should also be available to aid review, verification and approval. It is advisable to store each cost item in a database format for future use and enquiry.

Contingency

No base costs can be exact because of the variance which can occur during the life of a project, and because of areas which remain uncosted at project start. To overcome this problem it is standard practice to allocate a level of contingency. The standard method of doing this is to assess the risk associated with each item on the 'bill of quantities'. Once assessed, a contingency factor can be applied based on the individual characteristics of the item in question. Contingency cannot in truth be considered as a simple, across-the-board percentage though some companies do allocate it in this fashion.

With large projects, contingency allowance can amount to millions of pounds or dollars and therefore requires a method of control. The most common method in use is termed contingency rundown, a subject which we will discuss later (see p. 128).

Allocation of contingency is to a large extent a matter of experience. Probability and other analytical methods of calculating contingency, though theoretically sound, can have serious practical problems. The best method is therefore a blend of theory and practice. The contingency for each item once allocated, can then be aggregated, and the overall percentage calculated against the base element.

12.3   Cost integration and control

Part of the monitoring and control procedure is to monitor the cost elements in conjunction with accounts and planning. Planning will monitor and report the progress of the project, which is necessary for payments to be made and trends analysed to predict the future cost requirements. The accounts section will be required to monitor all payments and future commitments for financial calculations, tax and so on. Effective control requires a coding system which places a common identity code on groups of items. Cost engineering must therefore establish with planning and accounts a code of accounts which will meet as near as possible the monitoring requirements. The integration of the various codes is achieved by the generation of a cost breakdown code (CBC).

Cost breakdown code

The CBC should bring together the three basic codes used in control by relating them to a single code. There are a number of ways of developing this type of coded structure, using varying alpha numeric systems but all have the same common base. The following is one example of such a three-code structure:

- Code of accounts
- Activity code
- Cost code

Code of accounts

The code of accounts is normally allocated two digits, 01–99. This allows the accounts elements to be aggregated into major components. When required, a more detailed breakdown can be obtained through the use of the activity and cost codes. Today's computer software programs can develop the codes automatically (with a little help) but they still need guidance on the required breakdown. What follows may be regarded as a typical code breakdown.

Typical code of accounts listing

01   Management
02   Business management
03   Engineering and construction
04   Bulk materials
05   Equipment
06   Direct labour
07   Indirect labour
08   Services labour
09   Facilities
10   Transport
11   Special equipment
12   Fees
13   Miscellaneous

The actual codes used by a company may differ from the foregoing and may be more extensive but they do indicate the general principle.

Activity code

The activity code is related to the summary bar chart activities and therefore adds a timescale dimension to the costs with two digits normally sufficient to cover the key activities.

Typical activity code listing

Offshore structure

01 Design
02 Detailed engineering
03 Substructure
04 'A' Module
05 'B' Module
06 'C' Module
07 Civil works
08 Assembly module units
09 Outfitting
10 Testing and pre-commissioning
11 Transport components
12 Install components
13 Hook-up systems
14 Commission and handover

Process plant

01 Design
02 Detailed engineering
03 Civils
04 Process area 'aaa'
05 Process area 'bbb'
06 Process area 'ccc'
07 Off sites
08 Pipeline
09 Buildings
10 Hydro-testing
11 Transportation
12 Plant and equipment
13 Mechanical completion
14 Start-up

Cost code

The cost code is formed from three digits 001–999 to allow for the greater number of cost elements which must be considered. It is not intended for each nut and bolt to be given a cost code – only main categories are individually coded. Sub-codes can be used by individual departments such as purchasing in the form of invoice numbers to control the work but the costs should be able to be aggregated into a cost code category.

Using all three codes to their limit, we have the ability to break costs into 9 791 199 separate units which is more than is required for practical application or for general understanding. To list all the cost codes at this point is unnecessary but a typical breakdown of cost codes for one code of accounts would be as follows:

03 Engineering and construction – typical cost codes

050 Management and supervision
051 Structural

052 Electrical
053 Instrumentation
054 Piping
055 HVAC
056 Mechanical
057 Surface protection
058 Architecture/buildings
059 QA/QC
060 Civil

It should be noted that none of the lists of codes are intended to be complete but only to indicate the types and categories being considered.

From the examples shown, we may have a code structure as follows: **03/06/051** indicates that the costs are recorded against the structural elements of 'C' Module, and allocated to the engineering and construction section of the code of accounts. The code 03/06/051 indicates that the costs are recorded against the structure in process area 'ccc', and allocated to the engineering and construction section of the code of accounts.

As has been mentioned previously, many software packages are able to develop a code structure and link it through to cost/accountancy integrated packages. A common fault with any coding structure is that they can be extended through a 'thirst' for detail until it becomes almost a meaningless row of digits, only understood by a computer. This may be desirable or unavoidable if you are working in a supermarket with its thousands of products and you have the ability to operate a bar code system. But **project control requires the human element to comprehend the actions taken and have the ability to discern the outcome**.

No matter how good, large volumes of information are difficult to grasp in detail and lead to confusion within the mind of the average individual. In some respects the larger the project the simpler the detail must be. Assume for a moment that the human mind can hold and understand 100 bits of detailed information and the project has 1000 bits. The scope of each piece needs to cover 10 bits. If on the other hand the project has 30000 bits, then a piece must cover 300 bits. The bigger the project, the broader the brush.

Code generation

At the start of a project and during the tender or in the pre-tender phase, a draft set of codes should be developed to cover all the main functions.

These codes will give the cost engineer an initial starting point from which the budget can be built. As the initial project/tender progresses, the code structure can be developed both in breadth and detail to cover the evolving scope.

Computerisation of costs

Holding the coding structure in spreadsheet and database formats greatly facilitates the extraction and collation of information in a large number of alternative ways. The computer facility allows budgeted and actual costs to be analysed in greater detail, and provides the basic information for forecast analysis linking. An added advantage of computerisation is the ability to use sophisticated graphics packages to present even very difficult information in an easily understood way. If you have a point to make, if you want certain actions to be taken and decisions to be made by executives with limited time, use good graphics to get your information across.

12.4   Cost control: the basics

It is sad but true that cost control is a very limited exercise within too many of today's projects. What we do have, however, is a well-developed cost reporting and analysis vehicle which may be likened to a skier on a downhill run. We can measure his speed, plot his route with a high degree of certainty, know everything about the type of skis, clothing, snow and so on but can only watch as he goes over the precipice. Reporting was good, every twist and turn was seen on television, analysis was first-class, we predicted the exact route that was taken, and the exact time, within a few seconds as to when he would plunge to his death. A great job – or was it?

The point to remember is that reporting and analysis, though part of the control exercise, must never be confused with the control function. They are the vehicles by which the information is attained, and on which the control decisions are made.

Cost control has three basic components:

- Cost reporting
- Cost analysis
- Cost control

Cost reporting

Cost reporting relates to the gathering of information and presenting that information in a manner which can be subjected to further analysis.

The major aspect of the reporting will relate to progress measurement and forecast trends. For this information, the cost engineer will require the aid of the planning section. Due to the diversity of information required, touching on all aspects of the project, the cost engineer will involve all project functions. He will rely to a great extent on procurement and contracts for the actual expenditure and committed costs.

The cost report

The cost report will deal with all elements in the bill of quantities. It is therefore essential that the report is presented in a similar form to the bill of quantities for ease of comparison, segregation and analysis (see cost summary report). Cost reporting is an essential part of all projects as there is a basic need to give and receive payments. Unfortunately for many projects this is the only function performed.

Cost analysis

The cost analysis is the basic tool from which cost control directives can be generated. The techniques involved in the analysis relating specifically to the cost aspects used on a project are:

(A)   Value of work done
Normally presented in the form of an S-curve, this compares the value of work done according to the progress against that forecast at the start of the project, indicating whether progress is in keeping with costs to date. In the simplest of terms, at the 50% complete point of the project you may have planned to spend 70% of the project budget, due to purchase of materials. If you calculate you have now spent 80% of your budget, you have an overrun problem which needs to be explained and not only explained but used to forecast any further overspend trends.

When major budget overruns occur, the first question to be asked is: 'Was this not foreseen?'. If the answer is 'no', then we can only look for a degree of incompetence. If the answer is 'yes', then we must look to the management for the answer. Could it have been prevented, did they have the ability to prevent it, was the initial base estimate totally inadequate, was the potential overrun known and politically hidden? There are many questions which need to be answered and corrective action taken.

(B)   Cash flow forecast
The cash flow forecast is the principal management cost information document and should be presented in both tabular and S-curve form, indicating actual and forecast expenditure against income. In all cases, it should indicate the anticipated cost impact, individually and overall. For example, a minor item may increase by 300%, yet have little or no cost impact. Conversely, a major item may increase by 3%, and have considerable impact on the project budget. It is not the percentage overrun that is important, it is the cost impact on the project budget.

Overall budget cross-check

Before the project budget is finalised, an overall cross-check should be made against like products and projects. Any major deviations should be investigated for errors in the base estimate and on levels of contingency allocated. This is an expedient in the prevention of a significant base estimate error which could be the source of an immoderate overrun.

12.5   Contingency rundown

As the project progresses, contingency not now required should be returned to the company, reducing the company's need to hold much-needed funds against the project budget. One way to do this is to release contingency based on a contingency rundown curve.

Contingency rundown curve

With the allocation of costs and contingency to the scheduled activities, cost and contingency histograms including S-curves can be simply produced, similar to those used for manpower resources, only in this case using monetary values. This allows the progress of each activity to be shown and the planned and actual costs compared.

On the completion of each activity, the contingency expended can be assessed and plotted against the forecast rundown curve. Remaining contingency can then be rolled over, within specified limits, at the project manager's discretion to cover foreseeable problems, or returned to the company funds. **On no account can contingency be used which has been allocated to activities which are not yet in progress.** Contingency may be rolled forwards, but NOT backwards to cover/hide out-of-budget activities.

In the example as shown in Fig. 12.2, the remaining contingency percentage is plotted against the project progress percentage. Curve 'A' represents the derived contingency curve (normally shown as a percentage

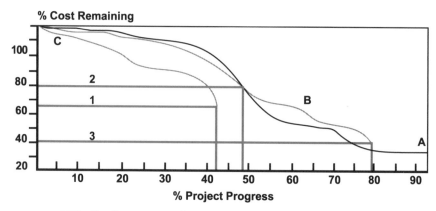

12.2   Contingency rundown.

for confidentiality). Curves 'B' and 'C' represent two possible examples of contingency used curves.

From curve 'B' we can see that the remaining contingency is maintaining a balance with the planned usage. Plot line 2 indicates that at the 50% progress point, funds could be returned to the company. Plot line 3 indicates that although 20% of the project and the contingency remains, contingency can still be rundown due to the lack of requirement.

Curve 'C' indicates a serious financial problem; contingency is being used up at a faster rate than planned, and would require an injection of funds or a management decision to use contingency reserved for future activities. Funds are available since contingency still remains but what about the future? It is now time to ring all the warning bells. Plot line 1 indicates that 45% of the contingency remains and 55% of progress has still to be achieved. At first sight this may look like a 10% negative deviation but if we examine the curve at this progress point, 70% of contingency should still be remaining. This indicates a 25% negative deviation which represents a much more serious problem. With what may be termed an ideal project, 100% contingency would remain to the project end and therefore even curve 'B' indicates the need for tight control to prevent an overrun of contingency.

Control of costs is a rapidly diminishing ability as a project develops, as the graph shown in Fig. 12.3 demonstrates.

One of the major influences on both contingency and cost control in general is cost commitment. Once the cost is committed, the funds may be

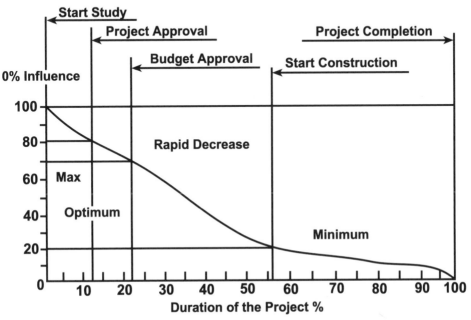

12.3   Cost control influence.

Budget %

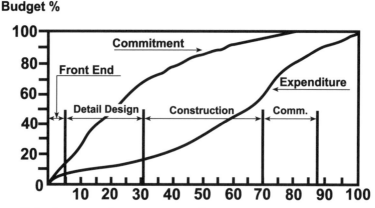

12.4   Cost commitment vs expenditure.

considered as expended although the actual expenditure will be some time later, as the graph shown in Fig. 12.4 indicates.

AFE (authority for expenditure)

One method of financial control which company management can and does adopt is the use of AFEs. AFEs allow the timely release and control of 'bulk' funds to the project and preclude the project management team from having to seek approval for every expenditure. The project budget, once established, is controlled with regard to expenditure by logically dividing it up into a number of AFEs for the timely release and control of funds by management.

AFEs may be set by the client as an external control mechanism, where an integrated client – contractor project management team are running the project. AFEs may also be set by the company as an internal control mechanism to regulate the company cash flow.

12.6   Cost reporting and control

The cost summary is the primary document in cost reporting. It is used to present the latest cost forecast, related to each activity-coded item. The most common form of the cost report is the spreadsheet format with column headings as follows:

A   Base estimate
B   Contingency
C   Project budget (A + B)
D   Approved variations

E   Scope changes
F   Current project budget (C + D + E)
G   Expenditure to date
H   Commitments to date
I   Estimate to complete
J   Final cost forecast (H + I)
K   Over- or underrun (C–J)

Vertical tabulation will indicate the project viability. Horizontal aggregation will indicate component viability.

Forecasting information

One of the main functions of a cost report is to forecast the final cost so that management can take early action, if necessary. In producing the cost forecast for the work in progress, and for work still to be undertaken, the cost engineer needs to evaluate in monetary terms. The planning analysis would or should contain the following information:

* Progress
* Productivity
* Man-hours
* Trends
* Probability
* Efficiency
* Durations

The planning analysis would be used to support the cost forecasts.

Early cost control

Cost control starts with the conceptual design in selecting a good practical concept requiring the minimum use of experimental technology. The next major step in controlling cost is the selection of a competent process/detail design contractor who will develop a good process solution. This will result normally in equipment/material savings with resultant cost savings. **Good design** in all its aspects from simple pipe layouts to the selection of specialised equipment **IS the most influential cost control factor**.

Contract awards and cost control

Contract awards can be the next most significant action in the control of costs. Knowledge and proven ability in contractor selection can be more significant than tender submission price. Contractor and subcontractor selection is of critical importance for long-term cost savings.

Cost control influence

At the start of any project, influence on the final cost and the project in general is at its highest. As ideas are firmed up as well as systems and equipment, control of the final outcome diminishes rapidly. We find that as we approach the area of maximum manpower utilisation i.e. construction, we have greatly reduced our cost-influencing ability. At the start of a project, it may be considered to be approximately 85%, diminishing to almost 20–25% by the start of construction.

From this we can see that 60% of cost control influence is lost during the design period due to the impact the design has on the final product and related costs. With only 20–25% remaining at the start of construction, great care must be exercised to make the best use of the diminishing control factor through good management and control. Without controls being established cost engineering becomes a 'bean counting' clerical function, and final project costs are in the lap of the Gods.

Remedial action

When the design is 'complete' and construction is underway, cost control is exercised by **taking remedial action in good time**. What the extent of that action will be will vary with the problem or potential problem. No problem should be viewed in isolation; each problem as it occurs requires forward impact analysis to ensure that no detrimental ramifications are excluded from the equation.

The cost of change increases rapidly as the project progresses. If a change is required or requested for whatever reason other than for issues of unsuitability or safety, that change must be evaluated under the following criteria:

- What will be the COST
- What will be the BENEFIT
- What will be the RISK INVOLVED

What must be avoided is preferential engineering, the 'nice to have' syndrome. It should be remembered that **there is no such thing as a change that has no cost or schedule impact** be it positive or negative. The cost may only be £1 and the time 5 minutes but they do exist. A very small change may still require input from engineering, QA/QC, and construction, which all takes time and effort. As for schedule impact, resources are diverted, be it only for an hour, from their scheduled task. In my experience I have known 'experts' at gathering changes of even the smallest magnitude and presenting the client with massive claims. A company supervisor thinking he or she is doing a good job asking for this and that to the 'expert' can and is a licence to print money.

Historical data – the basis for cost control

The value of good historical data cannot be overstressed because in our past lies the future. Time spent maintaining an extensive data bank on project performance, and drawing on that information for new projects, can prevent poor estimates. We may think that technology is moving so fast that historical data is of limited value. Technology *is* moving fast, equipment *is* improving by leaps and bounds in many fields but it is the detail that is changing with little change to the overall concepts. For example, a control valve may have gone through a major change but still requires the same 12 bolts to install it. An updated piece of electronic hardware may improve the working performance by 100% but may even take longer to install due to its complexity.

What we see in practical terms is that change in project performance is not an overnight transformation – it is a slow process.

By accessing good historical data at a project start-up, the cost engineer can establish with a fair degree of accuracy the potential problem areas, and the probability for success. Using this information, a realistic budget can be set.

12.7   Contractor/subcontractor tenders

We have discussed the need for good contractor selection as a major step in cost control, and this leads me to a small diversion – how to deal with tender submissions. The methods for dealing with contractor/subcontractor tenders and for maintaining security as part of the company/cost function are seldom defined.

It is essential that precautions are taken to maintain security with regards to tender price to ensure no unfair advantage can be gained by one bidder over another. This is a service not only to the company but to the bidder, who has spent time and money preparing his tender and who, therefore, does not want his efforts compromised.

Should a breach of security occur during the evaluation, the company would be answerable, not only to the senior company management, or client as the case may be, but more importantly, to the compromised subcontractor. To reduce the probability of a leak of vital information, certain standards of security precautions must be taken. The following is a guide to the security elements, which directly involves the cost engineer.

Bidder's tender documents

It is standard practice for the client/company to request the contractors on the tender list to submit their tender in a minimum of two volumes/sections.

Volume I would contain the commercial aspects and Volume II, and any subsequent volumes, the technical aspects. In practice certain features may occur in both volumes, when required for clarity, but no reference to money would be made in the technical section. This practice not only assists with overall security but does allow initial evaluations to be made on the commercial and technical aspects without one influencing the analysis of the other. The final analysis would naturally bring together both technical and commercial components.

Areas for analysis

In broad terms, there are five main areas which would require to be analysed and compared relating to any tender documents:

- Contractual elements
- Cost elements
- Contract co-ordination
- Engineering elements including QA
- Planning and scheduling

For the moment let us concentrate on tender security and how it would be maintained. What follows concentrates on the cost aspects but could well be applied to the entire evaluation.

Work area

Tender analysis must be conducted within a secure area, normally a lockable office, where entry is barred to all but the tender evaluation team. If the office has to remain open during the evening for cleaning, all desks should be cleared and all documents must be locked away.

Secrecy document (may be required by the client)

It is also common practice for a form of secrecy document to be signed by all members of the tender evaluation team. One of the main purposes of the document is to remind people of their security obligations.

Tender opening

Tender documents would be delivered to a specific location and before a certain time on a specified date. The tenders would be first opened at a precise time, and within the secure area, with specified key members of the tender evaluation team present. At this time the tenders (bids) would be split into their various sections, commercial and technical. A record would be maintained of who received what and when.

Working documents

The cost engineer must ensure that any and all tender documents in his or her possession remain locked away when not in use. He or she must also ensure that all calculations, notes and so on that have been made are kept in a working file with the **minimum** of loose paper. The engineer must ensure that when the office is unattended, **all** the documentation is secured under lock and key. (Limited loose paper makes this job easier.)

Duplication

If copies of any document must be made, the engineer must check that no copies or originals are left within the copy machine, and that all scrap is retained for disposal.

Scrap material

All scrap material, copies, notes, and calculations must be shredded before disposal.

Need to know

A cost engineer may require to seek advice from a third party outside the tender evaluation team. He or she should first obtain clearance from the team leader, and if granted, should make every effort to disguise the source of the question or document. The third party must be given only as much information as he or she needs to answer the question.

Telephone messages

It is standard practice to make only one contact person available to contractors or subcontractors. That person should note all questions, and reply by letter, telex, fax, cc-mail or e-mail, if appropriate. The question and answer will be copied to all contractors who are tendering.

Should contact be made direct to the cost engineer for whatever reason, the engineer should:

(a)   Transfer the call to the contact person
(b)   Should (a) not be possible, note the question, **give no answer** and ask the contractor to submit his question by fax or letter
(c)   Inform the contact person as soon as possible

Casual visitors

NO casual visitors should be allowed into the secure area.

Vulnerable area

The technical area is not subject to as high a level of 'spying' as the commercial area, which is more vulnerable due to the greater importance put on price information.

The cost engineer should be vigilant in maintaining his or her professional integrity with regard to security.

Planning co-ordination of contractors and subcontractors

13.1 Co-ordination procedures

As I look at proposal documents, tender submissions and contractor bid documentation there is a specific need to outline the basic requirements for planning proposals and submissions. Requirements for control and reporting are a key part of any proposal when a contractor is asked to bid. These requirements need to be specific, and to form part of the contract documentation. They are necessary for the successful integration of the contractor's planning and control system with the company's system.

In the case of planning, this requires the planning manager to make demands of the contractor with regard to the way he plans his work and the reports he produces. The closer they reflect the company system the easier and more efficient the integration will be.

The method of control used to achieve the integration/mirroring of systems is through a co-ordinating procedure which, as mentioned earlier, should form part of both the enquiry documentation and the subsequent contract. The following pages outline a typical co-ordination procedure applicable to any major project work item.

13.2 Proposal requirements

The proposal requirements give the bidder the first opportunity to assess what will be expected of him now and in the future. At this stage, the requests are specific but lack detail to allow the bidder a free hand to demonstrate his capability. *The questions being asked of him are: does he know what is involved in the project and does he have the skill to plan and control the work?*

Minimum requirements for proposal submission

- Procedures for planning, scheduling and progress monitoring
- Detail of facilities

- Project master network level 1, with resourced activities
- Summary bar chart
- Level I histograms
- Proposed sample documentation to meet company's requirements

Post-contract award schedule

As part of the integration of the contractor's programmes, schedules and reporting systems with the company's system, contractors are required to submit documentation conforming to the following essential elements:

- Project assignment code
- Project calendar
- Project monthly progress cut-off dates

Standard documentation

Standardising the documentation from the contractor/subcontractor is a major step forward in achieving integration. It is also a substantial time-saver by reducing interpretation time. The following is a typical outline of the minimum standard documentation which would be required.

Procedures

When submitting the proposals, the contractor will also submit for approval in principle, a copy of his detailed planning, scheduling and progress reporting procedures. *Does he have planning systems we can rely on to schedule and report progress on the work?*

Monthly report

The contractor should submit an example of a detailed monthly report covering all progress elements, based on project monthly progress cut-off dates.

Facilities

The contractor should, as part of his procedural documentation, prepare a basic philosophy and method statement. This document explains the implementation of his system to ensure the timely execution of the work. It should be complemented by, but not limited to:

- An organisation chart (for his own and subcontractors' staff)
- A list of key personnel to be used on the project, with CVs

- The computing facilities (hardware and software packages) intended for use on the project

Does he know how to use his system and does he have appropriate resources?

Logic networks

The method of logic networking for use on the contract will be Activity on Arrow or Precedence Networks.
Can he produce a proper logic network we can check and integrate?

Contracts networking levels

Three control and reporting levels will be used:

- Level I   Project master network
- Level II   Project control network
- Level III   Working networks/sub-networks

Mirroring the company system for better understanding and integration

To prevent any misunderstanding, the networking levels need to be explained in relation to the company's definition of the various levels. We have been over this ground before (see pp. 78–9 and 115–16), but as an aid to 'dipping' on chapters it is worth mentioning again.

Level I   Project master network

The project master network is designed as a tool to communicate all essential elements of the works and forms a key reporting document for summary reporting to senior management. Activities should be limited to approximately 50, and drawn in such a way as to be contained within one sheet.

The construction of the network shall be on a calendar base showing all key milestones, essential completion dates and so on. Updating shall be on a monthly basis and conform to the monthly progress cut-off dates. Monthly calendar divisions shall show the week starting Monday and contract calendar week number.

Level II   Project control network

The project control network is an amplification of the master network, and should contain 150–200 activities, establishing secondary elements and interim target dates for each of the master network activities. The updating of the control network shall be on a weekly basis with regard to progress, resources and logic. Manpower loading shall be shown on each activity. The network shall indicate mobilisation periods, interfacing with vendors/ suppliers, key and secondary milestones.

Level III   Working networks/sub-networks

Level III networking is intended to cover all sub-networks below level II. The extent of detail at level III shall be to suit the contractor's internal work allocation system.

The techniques described are fairly common and would present no difficulty to any major contractor or subcontractor. For a smaller contractor, the company will often provide guidance on the development of a good system. In my own experience, the high standard of planning and cost control we have today within many major and national companies is because of the demands made of them in planning and cost areas. There is little point in requesting information and not spelling out exactly what you want unless your contractors share your exact understanding of the subject or are first-class mind-readers. It is still true with most companies that 'If you don't ask, you don't get'! It is not in the contractor's interest either financially or politically to be overgenerous with their information.

More importantly, a request for additional reporting facilities after a contract has been signed can cost you money. Should you find at some later date that you do not need all the report functions you have contractually requested, you can always reduce your requirement and incur no financial burden.

Computer analysis of networks

The project control network, level II, should be used as the base for computer analyses of time, resources and cost. Computer analyses should contain as a minimum:

Time analysis

- Earliest and latest start of all design activities
- Actual start and finish dates of design activities
- Total float of all activities
- Critical path
- Sub-critical paths (sub-critical paths are defined as those with a total float of less than 3% or seven working days, whichever is the greater)

Resource analysis

- Based on early and late start
- Based on scheduled start
- By discipline
- By area and system

Trend analysis

- Overall progress – planned versus actual
- Manpower – planned versus actual
- By discipline
- By system

Should the contractor/subcontractor elect to use methods other than computer analysis, he will be required to generate the same level of information.

Again these demands should not be a problem to any contractor or sub-contractor of note but as mentioned earlier, if you don't ask for it, you may not get the information you need. If you ask for it later, you open the door to a cost claim.

13.3   Structure and regularity of reports

The following sections define how you wish the reports to be presented. Again, in my experience, you need to make clear your requirements or the information you request may be presented in a form which is of little value even though it still meets the contractual obligation.

Bar charts

The contractor will produce a summary bar chart for reporting purposes. The chart should be contained on an A3 format maximum. *At this time, it is advisable to give clear instructions of your exact requirements for the method of showing progress.*

Productivity reporting ('S' curves)

A separate productivity report, in graphical form based on man-hours expended, versus man-hours earned (as related to progress) shall be provided for the following:

- Project overall [Level I]
- Per discipline overall [Level I]

- Per design package [Level II]
- Per discipline [Level II]

Histograms

The contractor will produce histograms to complement the productivity reports listed above. The histogram calendar will coincide with the project cut-off dates. *Again it is important to ensure that the format presented contains the information you require.*

Manning report

The contractor will produce a weekly manning report for each activity in progress shown on the project control network, by discipline, including management and project services. The report should show the forecast of manning for the following four weeks. The report will include all subcontractor personnel employed in the execution of the works.

Man-hour summary report

A man-hour summary report will be submitted on a weekly basis conforming to the project cut-off dates, and containing the following details:

(a) Contract estimate at the time of contract award
(b) Man-hours expended to date
(c) Change in man-hour loading
(d) Revised estimate of man-hours i.e. (a) + (c)
(e) Forecast to completion
(f) Variance in man-hours i.e. (e) – (d)
(g) Earned man-hours (as related to progress)

Look-ahead schedule

The contractor will generate a four-week look-ahead schedule in the form of a bar chart, schedule or work list showing planned start and completion dates. The look-ahead schedule should be updated at two-week intervals.

The look-ahead schedule performs four functions i.e.:

- A check that the contractor is about to tackle the correct activities
- An early warning of plant and material requirements some of which you may be supplying

- Area access requirements and services facilities
- General resource information

13.4   Progress measurement

Progress measurement will be based on a physical measurement of work done, the progress being agreed between contractor and company. In cases of dispute, the company's decision shall prevail. The basis for measurement shall be the one used to calculate the original estimate. The measurement shall be assessed as a percentage of the activity weighting.

Activity weighting

To ensure a common base for all disciplines and ease of integration, progress weighted percentages will be based on planned man-hours unless agreed otherwise by the company.

NOTE: **Expended man-hours** shall not be accepted as a measurement of progress.
Earned man-hours shall be used to calculate productivity, i.e. hours earned versus hours expended.

Activity weighting forms the common ground for overall measurement. In the simplest of terms, if there were only two activities and one was complete, we could not say progress was 50% as one activity may be double the size of the other. Without activity weighting in some form, we would have no idea of the project's overall progress when hundreds of activities of various sizes are involved. Activity weighting allows us to calculate the progress of a major activity which may have a number of sub-activities, and relate it to the project as a whole.

Simplified example activity XYZ

Sub-activity A – 35 planned man-hours
Sub-activity B – 60 planned man-hours
Sub-activity C – 25 planned man-hours
Total   120 planned man-hours

Activity weighting

A =   29%
B =   50%
C =   21%
Total= 100%

From progress measurement activity A is 50% complete, B is 10% complete, and C is 100% complete, hence, the overall percentage complete can now be calculated:

$$A = 50\% \text{ of } 29\% = 14.5\%$$
$$B = 10\% \text{ of } 50\% = 5.0\%$$
$$C = 100\% \text{ of } 21\% = 21.0\%$$

Total and complete overall = 40.5%

With today's computer software, it is a simple matter to calculate the overall percentage complete for a whole project or any part of a project as long as the component activities can be aggregated. In the foregoing example, let us assume the total project was 12000 man-hours with the major activity XYZ valued as 1%. This would mean that activity XYZ contribution would be 0.405%. The principle is simple enough but in practice, with the thousands of project activities being progressed, the calculations are better left to the computer.

Incorporation of changes

To my knowledge, no major project has been undertaken without changes in scope occurring, and these cause the planned man-hours to change either up or down. Incorporating such changes, once approved, is fairly straightforward – the planned man-hours required for the change are added to or subtracted from the existing total of planned man-hours. The new total is then used as the basis for calculating percentage progress.

On a weekly basis, this may show a minor reversal on previous weeks' percentages complete, due to the increased work content. The progress narrative should highlight this point to prevent confusion.

13.5   Progress analysis and investigation

For those new to planning, cost engineering, or progress measurement let us take a few moments to go over a few of the basics again.

Planned man-hour

To effectively aggregate the total progress where mixed disciplines are involved, a common base must be established. That common base is the man-hour. For each activity to be undertaken, an estimate should be made of the man-hours necessary to complete the work. These man-hours are termed **planned man-hours.** By adding all planned man-hours together, the total planned man-hours for the project can be established.

The actual progress measurement i.e. 30% complete or whatever, would be measured using a tangible unit, metre of pipe, cubic metre of concrete, number of units installed and so on. Using these measurements the **earned man-hours** can be calculated i.e.

200 planned man-hours, 30% complete = 60 earned man-hours

Productivity can be calculated from the actual man-hours (**expended man-hours**) used to perform the work.

13.6 Progress investigation

Progress investigation is a major tool in the control of straying activities. It can identify at an early stage, errors in estimating, design faults causing construction difficulties, bad construction methods, low quality supervision, lack of materials or equipment, difficult working conditions, poor management and so on. Knowing the source of the problem will allow action to be taken to rectify the problem on future activities.

Progress investigation (sampling) should be undertaken when specific levels of progress are not attained or forecast, resulting in an overrun of the original activity duration. To be able to do this effectively we need a clear understanding of the following.

Sub-critical activities

The level of float (spare) time which will determine sub-critical activities depends on the overall duration of the contract, and the time required to take corrective action, if necessary. As an example of what is sub-critical and what is not, depending on the float available, assume you were driving to a meeting and you were unfortunate enough to have a punctured tyre. If you were very tight for time and only a few miles from your destination, the time taken to change the tyre could cause you to be late. On the other hand if you had allowed yourself a bit of spare time on your journey, a few minutes delay would present no problem.

What we learn from this simple example is that sub-criticality does not depend on the time taken, be it 10 minutes, 10 days or 10 months, but on the **impact that remedial action** would have on the float time available.

Productivity

'Productivity' in industry tends to be a misnomer because the efficiency which is actually being gauged is the accuracy of the activity man-hour estimate, the planned man-hours. An overestimated activity will show good productivity and an underestimated activity will show poor productivity for the same man-hours expended. However, the gauging of productivity does not lose its importance because of this but gains, in that the calculation of productivity and comparison of results over a period of time enables us to gauge the accuracy of the programme resources and durations. In this way, elements with low productivity can be identified and remedial action taken.

Calculation of productivity

Productivity is a function of **expended man-hours** and **earned man-hours**. Simple Example

Activity A – Planned man-hours = 200

– Progress = 30% complete
– Earned man-hours = 60

If the expended man-hours are 70 the productivity is simply calculated:

$$\text{Productivity} = \frac{\text{Earned man-hours}}{\text{Expended man-hours}}$$

$$= \frac{60}{70} = 0.86 \text{ (rounded up) or } 86\%$$

A simple calculation at this level, with a few hundred of activities to calculate is better left to the computer to number crunch. Progress deficiencies identified by discipline and examination of criticality plus a few pointed questions on deliveries and manning levels will normally expose any problem areas. The real difficulty arises in the taking of remedial action – it may even take courage, if that action impacts on senior management.

13.7 Authorised schedule changes

Project schedules shall only be revised when authorised by the company, and the consequential effects identified and reported. The approved project schedule is a contract document that is a promise as to when and how the work will be done. Special attention must be paid to critical and sub-critical items, target dates, milestones and completion dates. Schedule updates relating to progress and criticality should be once per week or at the request of the company.

Uncontrolled updates is an area that leads to a lot of confusion and lack of control if the contractor/subcontractor makes changes to his schedule that are not notified. Unfortunately, this does happen for many reasons, and keeping a tight control on changes is the only practical solution. Special vigilance should be taken if working on a computer network, where changes can be made easily and go unnoticed.

Instructions by company

The contractor shall comply with all specified instructions in order to maintain progress related to the approved work schedule. Note: *This instruction must be used with great caution. It is far too easy to make demands which may in fact impact negatively on the schedule. If this proves to be the case, it may prove to be the legal loophole to get out from under any completion liability.*

The contractor may be required to increase the number of operatives in a particular discipline or in his complete workforce. The contractor may also be required to increase his general facilities, level of management or adjust his procedures if the currently-approved work schedule is in jeopardy. This is more of a contractual obligation than a planning and cost one but needs to be stated if you are to keep control of the situation. Should you find you are able to relax the requirements in some areas, do it after the contract is signed – that way you can re-implement them without penalty.

Man-hour definitions

There are some people who, through lack of experience, may think that such control requirements are excessive. Experience has proved time and time again the need for detailed control definitions of this nature. It may seem simplistic but it is essential to ensure that all concerned have the same understanding of the definitions, as follows:

Planned man-hours

The number of man-hours envisaged to complete an activity and/or project.

Expended man-hours

The number of man-hours used on the activity irrespective of the progress.

Earned man-hours

The earned man-hour is a function of progress and planned man-hours.

e.g. Planned man-hours: 90
      Progress   50%
      Earned man-hours 45

Actual man-hours

Actual man-hours are the same as expended man-hours.

Paid man-hours

A paid man-hour is a man-hour for which the company is prepared to pay. Depending on the type of contract, it can be an earned man-hour or expended man-hour.

Productivity is: $\dfrac{\text{Earned man-hours or Actual man-hours}}{\text{Expended man-hours}}$

Clear definition of the various man-hours will enhance understanding of the various project documentation.

Design contractor progress monitoring and
measurement

14.1 Design – the progress nightmare

One of the first major contracts to be placed is for the design work – a contract element which presents difficulties of definition at any point in time due to the nature of the work. Its apparent lack of tangible units can send shivers through any progress monitoring team but by setting a few standards, we are able to provide guidelines as to what planning systems, procedures and progress measurement output should be expected from a design contractor.

14.2 Work content

In order to measure progress, it is necessary to estimate the work scope. With a design contractor, the main body of the work is tied up in calculation and the resultant drawings but, as we know, the estimate must be in units of measurement appropriate to the works, and capable of being recorded accurately as the work progresses.

14.3 Tangible units

Establishing the completion status of a particular activity is fundamental in the calculation of overall progress. Where possible, activity progress should be calculated in tangible units, i.e. a unit which can be physically measured. In the case of a design contractor, however, a tangible unit may be difficult to define.

We could try to estimate the total number of drawings of different sizes, and use that as a base – unfortunately, that would require some sort of sliding scale. An engineer may spend a week on calculations and a day on the drawing or the reverse – how do we compensate for this? With regard to the drawings and technical specifications, how is progress measured for these items and activities?

In truth, there is no exact way to measure progress with regard to design but we can come close to acceptable figures by using available historical data as to the number of documents and types required for a similar design. We will also have the experience of the estimated number of man-hours, documents, drawings and the like for the project design supplied by other bidders. Using such knowledge, it is possible to obtain a reasonable ball-park figure for the likely work content. The design contractor himself will not know exactly what the final scope may be but he will have made a best guess. Where the detailed scope of a contract is difficult to define, we can fall back on the logic network and the completion of specific major activities (milestones).

14.4   Milestones

Milestones are used to encourage the 'contracts' performance by with-holding payment for work done until a milestone has been achieved. The achievement of a milestone is a major step in progress, and as such, acts as a checkpoint for progress assessment. The design phase due to the number of unknowns is controlled by milestones covering the various scopes of work. Selecting the right milestone method is important.

There are three basic forms of milestones that could be used, depending on the type of work to be undertaken:

- Activity-defined milestones
- Progress-defined milestones
- Hybrid form

Activity-defined milestones

Where contract definition and work scope are **well defined**, milestones of this type can be set at key points throughout the duration of the contract, and would embrace specific key activities. This may be considered ideal, but has specific disadvantages in that the contractor or subcontractor has **no incentive to do work out of sequence** if so required, i.e. should the subcontractor find he is running out of work due to changes in design, lack of materials, there is a reluctance to start work for which payment may be extensively delayed. The contractor's planning will also be constrained and inflexible due to targeting present goals.

Progress-defined milestones

This system is the most flexible, and can be used where the scope is not well defined. It is similar to any standard progress payment system, but differs in that payments are made only on achieving pre-set goals, e.g. 20%, 40% or 60%. The milestone percentages are set at specific points, at which it is envisaged that certain key activities should be complete. Here, the contractor has an incentive, when directed by the company, to do work out of sequence should it be necessary to maintain economic working. The subcontractor's planning can be more flexible and more in keeping with his own working methods.

Hybrid milestones (defined progress initiatives)

This system is similar to the progress-defined milestone method, the difference being that key activities which have a major project impact are defined, and must be completed before payment is made for the milestone to which it relates.

This type of milestone is suitable for design contractors and contracts where information or activity completion is necessary for interfacing with other contractors and suppliers. Control and flexibility are maintained using this method. Where other contractors have to be brought in to do key work, which is linked to completion of a specific activity or activities, DPI has major advantages.

14.5 Progress measurement documentation

Progress of design documents can be estimated against a series of historical graphs showing the general flow and percentage tables, samples of which are shown below. A drawing or a document may be finished as far as the designer is concerned but the 100% completion can only be awarded when the work is approved for construction (AFC).

Engineering design can be broken down into various categories and weighting factors. The following is one example for a process plant:

• Basic design and process	9%
• Mechanical	6%
• Vessels	9%
• Piping	30%
• Electrical	10%
• Instrumentation	18%
• Civil	12%
• Structural	6%
Total	100%

The above breakdown can then be subdivided into smaller performance milestones as follows:

Piping and instrument drawings, plot plans		**Specifications, data sheets**
Prepare draft	10%	10%
Complete draft	20%	20%
Client review	10%	——
Internal review	20%	30%
Issue for approval	20%	20%
Client approval	15%	15%
Approved for construction	5%	5%

Procurement is closely aligned to design and can be progressed in a similar manner. Typical percentage breakdown and weighting factors may be as follows:

Procurement

Civils	5%
Steelwork	8%
Piping	8%
Mechanical	52%
Electrical	7%
Instruments	10%
Telecommunications	4%
Chemicals	2%
Buildings	4%
Total	100%

These weightings can then be subdivided into smaller performance milestones such as:

Drawings/specifications to vendor	20%
Processing quotations	20%
Approved for purchase	40%
Issue purchase order	20%
Total	100%

With fabricated items and equipment the smaller performance milestones would vary slightly i.e.

Purchase order issue	15%
Receive vendor drawings	5%
Start of fabrication	10%
Finish of fabrication	40%
Passed inspection and test	10%
Transportation	10%
Arrival on site	10%
Total	100%

Once agreement has been reached on the various breakdowns and overall quantities, progress measurement starts to become more realistic. It can never be perfect as the total scope by the nature of the function will not be known until the design phase is complete.

Predictions of the various interrelationships as a guide to judging the general flow of drawings, ISOs etc. can be ascertained by referencing historical trends as shown on Fig. 14.1–14.5.

One of the control tools to use here is activity weighting which is particu-

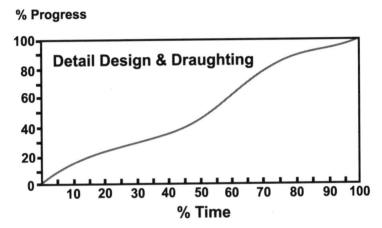

14.1   Overall progress curve.

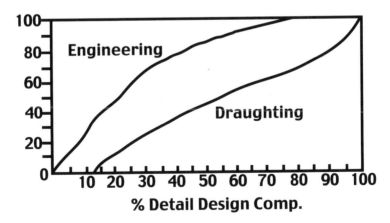

14.2   Design vs draughting.

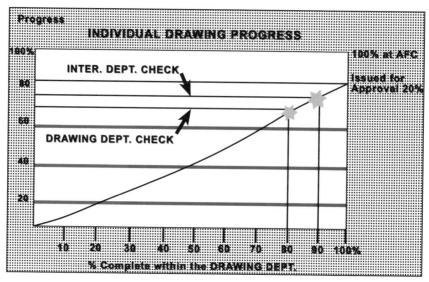

14.3 Drawing progress.

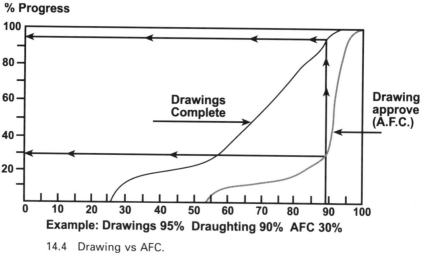

14.4 Drawing vs AFC.

larly important for a design contract as it has the ability to maintain a reasonable balance between simple drawings, specifications and the like, and difficult ones. We could say it has a 'swings and roundabout' effect but in practice it is more effective than that.

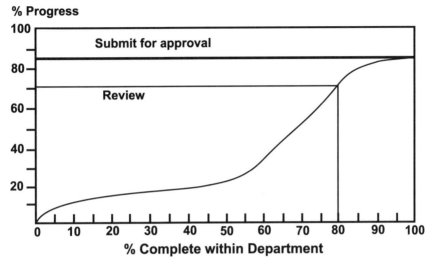

14.5   Preparing technical specifications.

A drawing being submitted for approval must not still require a substantial amount of work just to reap the benefit of the 80% complete progress payment. This must be stamped out at the first opportunity. It is also important from the client's point of view to ensure that he has sufficient people on hand to deal with approvals as quickly as possible.

The design phase is never easy; it is a time for decision-making, coupled with a heavy workload but in many ways it is the most satisfying.

15
Conclusion

The control of planning and costs in any major project is never an easy task. For those engineers who would hope one day to be the manager of a planning or cost section, it is important to remember that the job is not only technically complex, but requires a wide range of management skills.

For the benefit of those engineers who have recently taken over a management post, there are a few important things to remember. No matter how confident, or important, you feel within yourself, you are only one member of a team, and it is the team who will do the work. The job of the manager is not only technically demanding, but will require all your management skills to ensure that you get the best performance from your team.

Producing a good programme, complete with a realistic cost analysis and breakdown requires a high degree of skill. There is a delicate balance to be achieved within the schedule and cost parameters. An overestimation may prevent the award of the contract or the project proceeding. An underestimation may cost the company millions of pounds on a major project.

Major overruns are caused by one or all of the following: poor planning and cost estimating; inadequate control mechanisms; poor management; or, lack of contractor performance.

Dealing with these problems in reverse order, lack of contractor performance can be laid at the feet of those responsible for the selection of the contractor. The most important factor in selecting a contractor is their proven performance in the type of work to be undertaken.

This means that you must be very sure of your contractors. What work have they done, and how well did they do it? What work are they involved in now, and do they have sufficient resources remaining to meet your project demands? Do they have good project control tools?

If the only criterion for selection is cost, be prepared for problems. Be prepared to invest a lot of your time and your staff's time in supporting a contractor who has limited control techniques and resources.

Poor-quality management staff is something you may have inherited and have to live with. Your only course of action is to give them all the help and support you can, which you may feel is a waste of your time and energy. This is a natural reaction, but it does not solve the problem. Your goal is to bring the project to completion, in time and under budget, and it is your performance that matters, and that of the company as a whole. The targets which are achieved are a direct measurement of that performance.

Inadequate control mechanisms are a major fault on any project. Being without them is like sitting in a car which is doing 70 mph and then discovering that the steering, braking, and accelerator mechanisms do not work, and worst of all, you are locked in. As has been stressed in the book, you must ensure that you have good control tools, and know how to implement them.

One of the most important of these tools is good progress measurement and without it, your ability to forecast the future is severely limited. This limitation prevents you from taking in good time the corrective action which could remove or reduce a potential problem.

Poor planning and cost-estimating can be due to not knowing the scope of the work, limited ability, or both. Defining the scope of work to be undertaken is absolutely critical if you are going to plan or cost the work. If you do not know what has to be done, how can you plan or cost the work? It is that simple. Never expect the scope to be given to you on a plate, other than in broad terms. To establish the detailed scope will require a great deal of effort, understanding and experience. You do not have to be a genius to find out exactly what work has to be done – as mentioned once before in this book, genius is 1% inspiration and 99% perspiration – so be prepared to work at it!

With the best will in the world, there will be areas of work that will not be foreseen until they occur. If you have made the effort to define the scope well, these unforeseen additions will be limited, and will be contained within the contingency allocation. On the other hand if the scope has been under-defined, the undefined coupled with the unforeseen could result in a major overrun.

You need to remember that scope definition is not limited to just what must be done, but also how it will be done. A lack of understanding of how the work will be undertaken can, and often does, result in errors which can involve manpower, equipment, and time allocation, and all having an associated cost impact.

The only solution to the scope problem in all its aspects is to *ask* – in other words, make sure your communication channels are wide open. Do not let any aspect of the project that you do not fully understand go unquestioned, even if you feel that you are asking a foolish question. You will find most people who are good at their job are pleased to help, as it gives them an opportunity to demonstrate their knowledge and ability in their particular field.

Good planning is based on the practical application of the knowledge gained, with regard to the extent of the project scope. The scope, and the work related to the scope, once processed and analysed, forms the basis for a workable plan. It is from this plan that the cost engineer will derive the resource costs and cost profile.

In the case of a department with limited ability, or lacking the depth of experience required to handle a major project, it is the manager's primary responsibility to head off, and to find a solution to, any potential problems. It is not always easy to do this as there can be a natural resistance from a manager to finding fault with his or her own team members, and even more so, with himself! Resolving the problem may involve making a greater coaching effort, using one's own knowledge and expertise to improve the performance of the team.

It may be a case of bringing in additional staff with the relevant experience to work with the team. There may be a case for certain members of the team to be sent on an external training course to improve their management skills.

The solutions required could be as numerous as the number of staff the manager has within the department or section but if a problem exists in whatever sphere of the project and is impacting on performance, *don't live with it, find the solution.*

I have briefly discussed the problem with projects which overrun their schedule and budget to a dramatic extent but we should not forget those projects which get it right. Unfortunately, getting it right tends to be taken for granted – a nice dinner at the end of the project, a few speeches, and it's on to the next one. This is a pity because, in some ways, the project staff and management are unsung heroes, people doing a job the best way they can and doing it well. In today's world, this is not an easy task.

To bring a project to its completion inside the planning and cost parameters requires not only a realistic plan and budget but also the dedication of all those involved in a project. No major project is undertaken without problems arising – that's the 'nature of the beast' – but a good project team will take them in their stride and find solutions which will lessen their impact on the schedule and related costs.

The advantage of good engineering, construction and support disciplines should not be underestimated, as they are the people who are doing the physical work. Often, the action taken by competent discipline engineers in the field will overcome problems, reducing, or nullifying the impact on the cost and schedule.

Those projects which do achieve their targets demonstrate the ability of the project team as a whole to work together towards the fulfilment of the project goals.

The range of major projects is increasing every year. As technology advances, we increase our ability to tackle projects that would not have been considered a decade ago. These new projects will make greater and greater demands on the planners and cost engineers. There will be major areas where there is no historical data to use as a base. Often the planning and cost aspects will have to be based on the best educated guess.

The only advice that can be given is, bring to bear all the knowledge and experience you can, and all the tools at your disposal. I hope that this book will be one of them.